Human–Computer Interaction Series

SpringerBriefs in Human-Computer Interaction

SpringerBriefs in Human-Computer Interaction presents concise research within the fast growing, multidisciplinary field of Human-Computer Interaction (HCI). Designed to complement Springer's prestigious *Human-Computer Interaction Series*, this Briefs series provides researchers with a forum to publish cutting-edge scientific material relating to any emerging HCI research that is not yet mature enough for a volume in the *Human-Computer Interaction Series*, but which has evolved beyond the level of a journal or workshop paper.

SpringerBriefs in Human-Computer Interaction are shorter works of 50–125 pages in length, allowing researchers to present focused case studies, summaries and introductions to state-of-the-art research. They are subject to the same rigorous reviewing processes applied to the *Human-Computer Interaction Series* but offer exceptionally fast publication.

Topics covered may include but are not restricted to:

User Experience and User Interaction Design
Pervasive and Ubiquitous Computing
Computer Supported Cooperative Work and Learning (CSCW/CSCL)
Cultural Computing
Computational Cognition
Augmented and Virtual Reality
End-User Development
Multimodal Interfaces
Interactive Surfaces and Devices
Intelligent Environment Wearable Technology

SpringerBriefs are published as part of Springer's eBook collection, with millions of users worldwide and are available for individual print and electronic purchase. Briefs are characterized by fast, global electronic distribution, standard publishing contracts, easy-to-use manuscript preparation and formatting guidelines and have expedited production schedules to help aid researchers disseminate their research as quickly and efficiently as possible.

More information about this subseries at http://www.springer.com/series/15580

Haiyue Yuan • Shujun Li • Patrice Rusconi

Cognitive Modeling for Automated Human Performance Evaluation at Scale

Haiyue Yuan
Centre for Vision, Speech, and Signal Processing
University of Surrey
Guildford, Surrey, UK

Shujun Li
School of Computing
University of Kent
Canterbury, Kent, UK

Patrice Rusconi
School of Psychology, Department of Psychological Sciences
University of Surrey
Guildford, UK

ISSN 1571-5035 ISSN 2524-4477 (electronic)
Human–Computer Interaction Series
ISSN 2520-1670 ISSN 2520-1689 (electronic)
SpringerBriefs in Human-Computer Interaction
ISBN 978-3-030-45703-7 ISBN 978-3-030-45704-4 (eBook)
https://doi.org/10.1007/978-3-030-45704-4

This Springer imprint is published by the registered company Springer Nature Switzerland AG
The registered company address is: Gewerbestrasse 11, 6330 Cham, Switzerland

Contents

List of Figures

List of Tables

Chapter 1
Introduction

Abstract Cognitive models and related software tools have been developed to study human cognitive processes such as perception, memory, and attention to better understand human mind, as well as model and simulate human behaviors. Although they have been widely used and proved to be very useful, there are some challenges preventing large-scale modeling and simulation tasks from being conducted efficiently and effectively.

To discuss and address these challenges, in this book, we aim to provide readers an overview on relevant subjects such as cognitive architectures, cognitive models, and related software tools for modeling and simulation. In addition, we would like to demonstrate the use of human behavioral data to facilitate the cognitive modeling process. Furthermore, we present our recent work on a new conceptual framework for supporting large-scale cognitive modeling, and introduce a research software prototype with example use cases.

In the first chapter of the book, we firstly present a brief overview of cognitive modeling and human performance evaluation with potential challenges and issues, followed by a summary of other chapters of the book. This chapter ends with listing the main objectives and main target audience for this book.

1.1 Cognitive Modeling and Human Performance Evaluation

Many cognitive models have been proved effective and useful to evaluate human performance. Particularly, cognitive models following the GOMS (Goals, Operators, Methods, and Selection) rules [7] have attracted lots of interest from both researchers and practitioners especially user interface (UI)/user experience (UX) designers in different sectors. Such models can predict human performance of conducting computer-based tasks, therefore helping researchers and practitioners to design and refine user interface (UI) designs without conducting time-consuming user studies and full prototyping [6].

H. Yuan et al., *Cognitive Modeling for Automated Human Performance Evaluation at Scale*, Human–Computer Interaction Series,
https://doi.org/10.1007/978-3-030-45704-4_1

To better facilitate and simplify the modeling process, psychologists and computer scientists have worked together to develop a number of software tools (e.g., CogTool [8], SANLab-CM [10], Cogulator [14]). These tools can reduce manual work involved in the modeling process and automate the simulation process. However, challenges and issues have been identified for modeling complex and dynamic tasks/systems [4, 11, 12, 16], and in many applications there is a need to integrate additional data source to facilitate modeling process at a large scale using existing software tools (such as work reported in [15]). Chapter 3 of this book reviews some existing open source cognitive modeling software tools and summarizes and discusses some of these identified issues and challenges in details. To provide solutions to these challenges and issues Chaps. 4 and 5 of this book present our work on a conceptual framework, and developing a research prototype of the framework for supporting modeling human performance at large scale, respectively.

1.2 Overview of the Book

The rest of the book is organised as following:

- Chapter 2 presents background information and brief overview about cognitive approaches to Human Computer Interaction (HCI) including cognitive architectures (e.g., ACT-R [1, 2], SOAR [9], and CLARION [13]) and cognitive models (GOMS [7], KLM [3], and CPM-GOMS [5]).
- Chapter 3 provides a review of open source cognitive modeling software tools. This chapter also lists a number of case studies of using these software tools in both HCI and cyber security domains, followed by discussing issues and challenges of using these tools to model complex tasks/systems at a large scale.
- Chapter 4 firstly provides an overview on the integration of behavioral data into the cognitive modeling process, followed by presenting two user studies of integrating eye tracking data to better understand and model human behaviors of using cyber security systems.
- Chapter 5 presents our recent work on a conceptual framework called CogFrame to automate large-scale cognitive modeling tasks, and how we developed CogTool+ – a research prototype following the conceptual framework.
- Chapter 6 uses three concrete use cases to demonstrate how CogTool+ can be used to simplify the processes of modeling and simulating complex systems at large scale.
- Chapter 7 summarizes key findings of each chapter, and concludes this book with a discussion of possible future work.

1.3 Who This Book Is For?

This book is mainly for HCI/UI/UX researchers, designers and practitioners. Nevertheless, this book contains multi-disciplinary research studies, and people from different domains can benefit from this book. This book contains a review of state-of-the-art open source cognitive modeling and simulation software tools and their applications. Researchers and practitioners working on subjects such as psychology, HCI, and cyber security may find interesting topics throughout this book.

This book also presents examples of integrating cognitive psychology and computer science to study HCI issues/topics, as well as demonstrating how empirical data (i.e., particularly eye tracking data) can be collected and fed into the development of a new research software prototype for cognitive modeling and simulation. This could potentially attract interests from psychology and computer science researchers.

Furthermore, this book introduces a novel conceptual framework that allows (semi-)automated large-scale modeling and simulation of human cognitive tasks. An open source software (a research prototype) has been developed based on this framework, thereby audience of this book can benefit from theoretical knowledge as well as having hands on practical experience.

References

1. ACT-R Research Group: ACT-R. http://act-r.psy.cmu.edu/ (2016). Accessed: 25 Aug 2016
2. Anderson, J.: How Can the Human Mind Occur in the Physical Universe? Oxford University Press, Oxford (2007)
3. Card, S., Moran, T., Newell, A.: The keystroke-level model for user performance time with interactive systems. Commun. ACM **23**(7), 396–410 (1980)
4. De Luca, A., Hertzschuch, K., Hussmann, H.: Colorpin: securing pin entry through indirect input. In: Proceedings of the SIGCHI Conference on Human Factors in Computing Systems, CHI'10, pp. 1103–1106. ACM, New York (2010). https://doi.org/10.1145/1753326.1753490
5. Gray, W.D., John, B.E., Atwood, M.E.: The precis of project ernestine or an overview of a validation of goms. In: Proceedings of the SIGCHI Conference on Human Factors in Computing Systems, CHI'92, pp. 307–312. ACM, New York (1992). https://doi.org/10.1145/142750.142821
6. Gray, W.D., John, B.E., Atwood, M.E.: Project Ernestine: validating a GOMS analysis for predicting and explaining real-world task performance. Hum. Comput. Interact. **8**(3), 237–309 (1993)
7. John, B., Kieras, D.: The GOMS family of user interface analysis techniques: comparison and contrast. ACM Trans. Comput.-Hum. Interact. **3**(4), 320–351 (1996)
8. John, B., Prevas, K., Salvucci, D., Koedinger, K.: Predictive human performance modeling made easy. In: Proceedings of the SIGCHI Conference on Human Factors in Computing Systems, CHI'04, pp. 455–462. ACM, New York (2004). https://doi.org/10.1145/985692.985750
9. Laird, J.: The Soar Cognitive Architecture. MIT Press, London (2012)

10. Patton, E.W., Gray, W.D.: Sanlab-cm: a tool for incorporating stochastic operations into activity network modeling. Behav. Res. Methods **42**(3), 877–883 (2010). https://doi.org/10.3758/BRM.42.3.877
11. Roth, V., Richter, K., Freidinger, R.: A pin-entry method resilient against shoulder surfing. In: Proceedings of the 11th ACM Conference on Computer and Communications Security, CCS'04, pp. 236–245. ACM, New York (2004). https://doi.org/10.1145/1030083.1030116
12. Sasamoto, H., Christin, N., Hayashi, E.: Undercover: authentication usable in front of prying eyes. In: Proceedings of the SIGCHI Conference on Human Factors in Computing Systems, CHI'08, pp. 183–192. ACM, New York (2008). https://doi.org/10.1145/1357054.1357085
13. Sun, R., Slusarz, P., Terry, C.: The interaction of the explicit and the implicit in skill learning: a dual-process approach. Psychol. Rev. **112**(1), 159–192 (2005)
14. The MITRE Corporation: A cognitive modeling calculator. http://cogulator.io/ (2014). Accessed: 25 Aug 2016
15. Yuan, H., Li, S., Rusconi, P., Aljaffan, N.: When eye-tracking meets cognitive modeling: applications to cyber security systems. In: Human Aspects of Information Security, Privacy and Trust: 5th International Conference, HAS 2017, Held as Part of HCI International 2017, Vancouver, 9–14 July 2017, Proceedings. Lecture Notes in Computer Science, vol. 10292, pp. 251–264. Springer, Cham (2017)
16. von Zezschwitz, E., De Luca, A., Brunkow, B., Hussmann, H.: Swipin: fast and secure pin-entry on smartphones. In: Proceedings of the 33rd Annual ACM Conference on Human Factors in Computing Systems, CHI'15, pp. 1403–1406. ACM, New York (2015). https://doi.org/10.1145/2702123.2702212

Chapter 2
Cognitive Approaches to Human Computer Interaction

Abstract This chapter presents a brief overview of theories and concepts that arsome well-established and widely used cognitive architectures, such as ACT-R (Anderson et al (2004) Psychol Rev 111(4):1036–1060; Anderson (2007) How can the human mind occur in the physical universe? Oxford series on cognitive models and architectures. Oxford University Press, Oxford) and SOAR (Laird (2012) Soar cognitive architecture. MIT Press, Cambridge). These are computational attempts to model cognition for general and complete tasks rather than for single, small tasks. This chapter also reviews the most known and used cognitive models, KLM and GOMS, which are computational models used for simulations of human performance and behavior (Ritter et al (2000) ACM Trans Comput-Hum Interact 7(2):141–173. https://doi.org/10.1145/353485.353486). We will show how some cognitive architectures that originated within artificial intelligence (AI) have been developed to cover aspects of cognitive science, and vice versa. The relevance of the cognitive approach to HCI can be seen in the successful use of cognitive models in the HCI community to evaluate designs, assist users' interactions with computers, and substitute users in simulations (Ritter et al (2000) ACM Trans Comput-Hum Interact 7(2):141–173. https://doi.org/10.1145/353485.353486).

2.1 Cognitive Architectures

Cognitive architectures are general theories of human cognition that address the issue of how human mind is instantiated in the physical brain. They detail cognitive mechanisms relatively regardless of the implementation level [3, 5, 29, 43]. This approach to cognitive modeling of human behavior is "low level" because it focuses on the steps encompassed by perceptual, motor, cognitive, and, more recently, neural processes aiming at modeling a complete and complex process rather than a single, small task [6, 28, 39, 43].

It is thus an attempt to reach a coherent and unified view of human cognition [2, 20, 30]. There are several reviews and classifications of cognitive architectures [18, 19, 34, 43]. For the purpose of this brief review, we will classify them as sym-

H. Yuan et al., *Cognitive Modeling for Automated Human Performance Evaluation at Scale*, Human–Computer Interaction Series,
https://doi.org/10.1007/978-3-030-45704-4_2

bolic, sub-symbolic, and hybrid. Symbolic architectures entails the manipulation of symbols, that is, entities that can be linked to one another, stored, retrieved, and selected by means of rules that can also trigger action selection and execution. Sub-symbolic architectures represent concepts across multiple nodes in a network such as in parallel distributed processing (PDP) models [36]. Hybrid architectures combine symbolic components, such as rules, and sub-symbolic components, such as activation values [34].

This section briefly reviews some widely used cognitive architectures and their applications. In particular, the focus will be on the hybrid architectures Adaptive Control of Thought – Rational (ACT-R) [5], and SOAR [21], which in their revised versions [22], have both symbolic and sub-symbolic components. While ACT-R originated in cognitive science and focuses on behavioral data (e.g., about human memory), it has then been extended to cover aspects related to artificial intelligence. SOAR originated in the artificial intelligence field and it focuses on the functional capabilities of the architecture and intelligent agents, but it has then been extended to cover aspects of cognitive science [20, 34].

2.1.1 ACT-R

ACT-R is a cognitive architecture that aims at specifying the mechanisms of how the human mind works, but it is also a piece of software. Its origins can be traced back to the theory of Human Associative Memory (HAM) by Anderson and Bower (1973) [34, 43]. HAM was an associative theory of memory that, compared to previous associative theories, gained precision by being formalised through a List Processing (LISP) code that allowed for computer simulation [1]. HAM does not specify how memories are used in cognitive processes, and the ACT (Adaptive Control of Thought) model represents a development of this theory that filled this gap [1]. Indeed, the ACT model encompasses a procedural system of knowledge representation (i.e., a memory system that includes knowledge of, for example, how to drive a car or to play the piano) that is linked to a memory system derived from HAM [1]. The other system of model representation in ACT is the declarative memory system, that includes memories of facts such as who was the first president of the United States. Scholars have developed several versions of the ACT model throughout the decades. In particular, the integration of Anderson's rational analysis of cognition led to the Adaptive Control of Thought – Rational (ACT-R) model [4, 34, 43].

ACT-R uses units of knowledge called chunks [2] that are stored in and retrieved from the declarative memory, and production rules (if-then rules that allow the model to act based on a condition [34]) for the procedural system. Productions are the symbolic component of ACT-R. The processes that determine the priority among different productions, the utility of a chunk (based on its recency and frequency, and the context) and the learning mechanisms are captured by the sub-symbolic component of ACT-R. Sub-symbolic processes can be instantiated by setting the utility parameters of productions and activations (numeric values) [2].

ACT-R is made up by a series of modules that work in parallel. However, some processes are serial. The modules can produce only one outcome at a time and only one production fires at any given time [20]. The modules operate around a central production system that processes the information (i.e., chunks) placed by the modules in buffers. These are the interface between the production system and the modules as well as the environment. When information in the buffers is recognized, a production fires, and then the buffer is updated. The minimum time assumed to complete this cycle is 50 ms [2]. The main modules in ACT-R are: the intentional module, that holds the information about the current goal, the declarative module, that retrieves information from the declarative memory, the visual module, that holds information about object identity and location, and the manual module for motion [2, 3, 20, 34] (Fig. 2.1).

Learning mechanisms in ACT-R include: spreading activation, partial matching, blending, and production compilation [23, 32]. Spreading activation is based on the strength of association that leads the chunks in the buffers to spread their activation to the chunks in the declarative memory. Partial matching is based on the retrieval of chunks that are similar to those previously retrieved. Blending

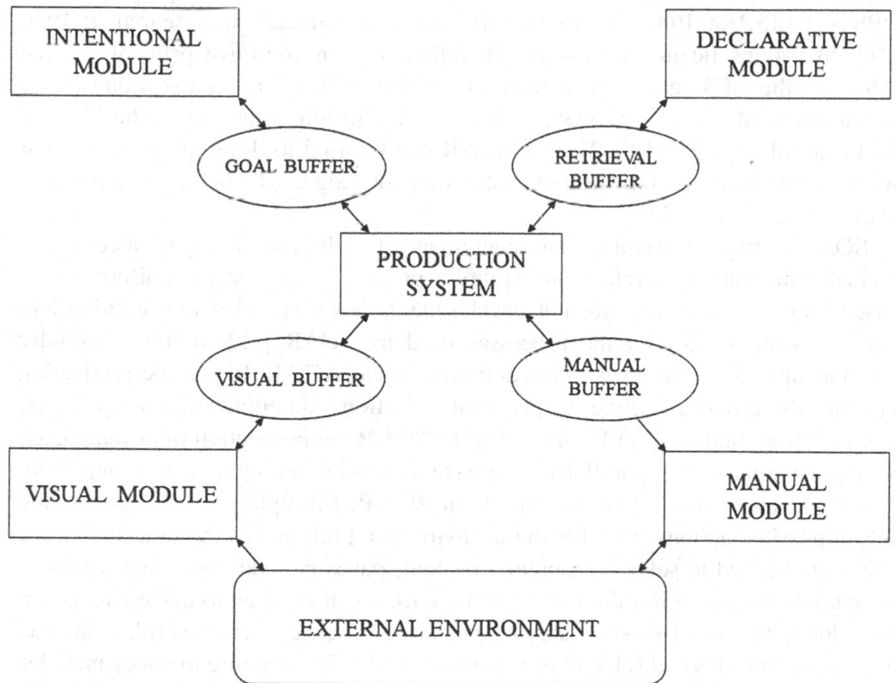

Fig. 2.1 Representation of the modular structure of ACT-R based on [2, 20, 34]

entails a retrieval of a mix, an "average" of all chunks. Finally, collapsing two production rules can lead to the acquisition of a new production rule through the mechanism of production compilation [34]. Recently, ACT-R has been mapped into brain correlates of cognitive processes, the "Brain Mapping Hypothesis" [5, 6, 26].

ACT-R has been used to model several human behaviors [34]. For example, it has been used to model driving behavior [37] and the effects of being distracted while driving [38], intuitive decision making [14], human behavior when faced with a phishing attack [44], eye and head movements in environments with multiple monitors [31], information selection in simulated geo-spatial intelligence tasks [32], and decision making in dynamic settings [45]. Accordingly, ACT-R is one of the most widely known and used cognitive architectures.

2.1.2 SOAR

The SOAR (State, Operator, And Result) cognitive architecture represents a functional approach to understanding what cognitive mechanisms underlie human intelligent behavior [21, 35, 43]. In particular, the aim of its developers is to build "human-level agents", that is, computational systems that have the same cognitive capabilities as humans [22]. SOAR was introduced as a computer program using OPS and LISP in 1982, but its origins can be traced back to research in 1956 [21]. Its origins lie in the field of AI, rather than in cognitive psychology like HAM for the ACT model. It focuses on problem solving mechanisms and it is a development of the first AI system able to solve different problems, the General Problem Solver (GPS) [22, 27, 43]. SOAR can be used to develop AI agents that solve problems based on different types of knowledge, whether programmed or learnt by the system [22].

SOAR's original development encompassed only one learning mechanism (called "chunking"); it relied on symbolic processes only, and a uniform, rule-based long-term memory. Recent developments have extended the learning and memory systems as well the processes used by SOAR [22]. It has a modular structure and two main types of memory systems as ACT-R. It is a rule-production system, whereby rules define the proposal, selection, and application of operators, that is, actions and goals [13]. In contrast to ACT-R, all production rules that match at a given time fire in parallel [22]. Production rules incorporate the long-term, procedural knowledge of the system as in ACT-R. Multiple *problem spaces* (the sets of possible actions available in the environment relevant to the task) define the behaviors needed to solve a problem. Problem spaces include *states* that represent the current progress toward the goal, and *operations* that allow to make changes in the solution process. Decisions are made through a cycle governed by rules that lead to changes in states and selections of operators. SOAR's working memory includes declarative structures about the states as well as the operators that are proposed and currently selected [22]. The selection of an operator occurs by means of the

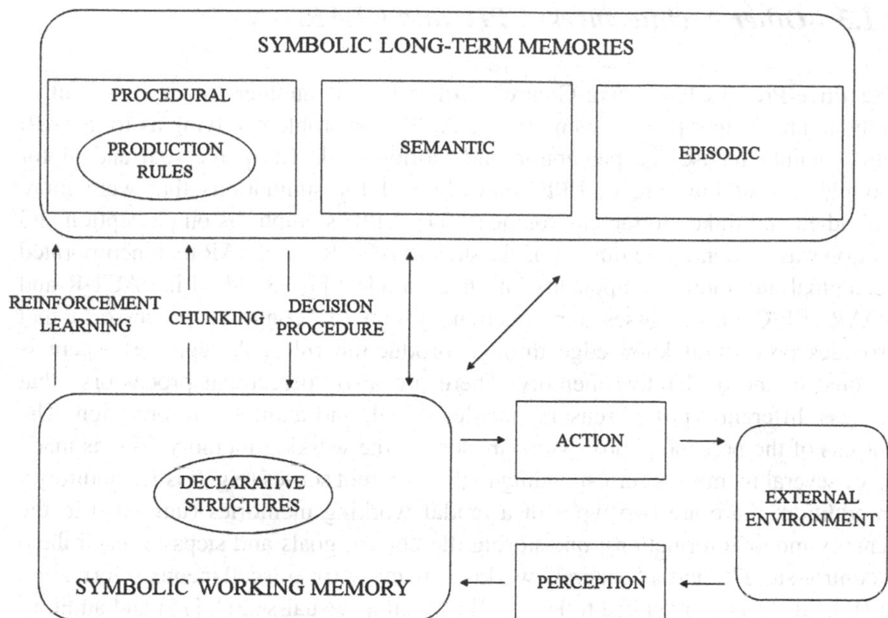

Fig. 2.2 Representation of the modular structure of SOAR based on [22] and [20]

decision procedure based on some *preferences* created by the production rules. Operator selection is followed by operator application that determines changes in the working memory. Those changes can trigger either retrievals from semantic (facts about the world and the available actions) and episodic (e.g., when past actions were executed) memories or interactions with the external environment. Beyond chunking, that allows the acquisition of new production rules, learning in SOAR can occur by means of reinforcement learning, that acts on the production rules that generate the preferences to select the operators [22, 35] (Fig. 2.2).

Based on ACT-R's activations, SOAR includes sub-symbolic processes in the way items in the working memory are associated with different activations based on the recency and frequency of use to give them different importance [22].

SOAR has been applied to many domains, which can be classified in four categories: expert systems (e.g., medical diagnosis), cognitive models (e.g., learning in HCI), autonomous agents, and models of human behavior [22]. An example of the largest application of SOAR form the last category is TacAir-SOAR used in the simulation of large-scale military flight missions to generate behaviors similar to those performed by human pilots while in flight [13, 43]. At the basis of this large-scale simulation system there is a hierarchy of operators (e.g., goals) that are simplified by additional operators until the action execution [13, 43].

2.1.3 Other Architectures: EPIC and CLARION

Executive-Process Interactive Control (EPIC) [25] is another low-level cognitive architecture. Rather than on memory like ACT-R or problem solving as for SOAR, EPIC mainly focuses on perception and motion [43]. The perceptual and motor modules are at the core of EPIC and allowed for simulations that were more embodied and linked to the environment [34]. EPIC's emphasis on perception and motion was influential for other models, such as ACT-R and SOAR that incorporated perceptual and motor components into their models [7, 33, 34]. Like ACT-R and SOAR, EPIC encompasses a production system (a "cognitive processor") that provides procedural knowledge through production rules. A separate system is devoted to the declarative memory. There are also "perceptual processors" that process different types of sensory (tactile, visual, and auditory) information. The outputs of the perceptual processors are sent to the working memory. This is made up of several memories corresponding to the different senses (e.g., visual, auditory). In addition, there are two types of a modal working memories (unrelated to the sensory-motor information): one storing the current goals and steps to reach them ("control store"), and a "general" working memory for miscellaneous information [17]. EPIC has been applied to HCI [17] as well as visual-search [15] and auditory tasks [16] with implications for system design.

Although cognitive architectures provide details on cognitive mechanisms independently of a specific implementation, some of them rely more strongly than those we have reviewed so far on the implementation level discussed by Marr [24], such as the neural processing [43]. An example of these types of cognitive architectures is CLARION, which relies on connectionist and neural networks [11, 41]. CLARION assumes that there are two types of knowledge, implicit and explicit, that interact. Representations of both types are used by both the procedural memory (the "action-centred" subsystem, that is also used for some executive functions) and the declarative memory (the "non-action-centred" subsystem). Two additional subsystems, the motivational and the meta-cognitive ones, have control over the action-centred and the non-action centred subsystems [40]. Examples of processes modeled using CLARION are human reasoning [42] and creative problem solving [11].

2.2 Cognitive Models

This section presents a brief overview of theoretical concepts for cognitive modeling that are relevant to this book, especially Chaps. 5 and 6. We hope that the audience can learn some theoretical and conceptual knowledge after reading this section before reading more technique details about our approach of developing a conceptual framework and a cognitive modeling tool for supporting automated human performance evaluation at large scale.

One of the most widely known theoretical concepts in HCI is GOMS analysis, which can provide insightful knowledge of human performance task in terms of **G**oals, **O**perators, **M**ethods, and **S**election rules [12]. Since its publication, many variants of the GOMS, and related software and applications have been developed in both research and commercial communities. Here we present an overview of three main variants – GOMS, KLM, and CPM-GOMS – for the rest of this section.

2.2.1 GOMS

GOMS was introduced in the book 'The Psychology of Human Computer Interaction' written in 1983 by Stuart K. Card, Thomas P. Moran and Allen Newell [9]. GOMS was defined as "a set of **Goals**, a set of **Operators**, a set of **Methods** for achieving the goals, and a set of **Selection rules** for choosing among competing methods for goals".

- *Goals* represent the goal that the user wants to achieve by using the system/software/user interface. Normally, the goal consists of a number of sub-goals, where all sub-goals must be accomplished in sequence to achieve the overall goal.
- *Operators* are actions performed to achieve the goal, where actions can be perceptual, cognitive, motor, or etc. Operators are most likely to be defined at a concrete level, such as the button press event, the menu selection, and etc. Execution time is one of the important parameters of the operator, which is assumed to be independent of how the user/system moved to the current state [12]. The accuracy of the GOMS predicted performance time depends on the accuracy of the execution time. The execution time could be estimated from a statistical distribution, or calculated as a constant, or derived using a mathematics function.
- *Methods* are sequences of operators and sub-goals to achieve a goal, where the content of the methods is determined by the operators.
- *Selection rules* is used when there is more than one method to achieve a goal. The decision of selecting a specific method can be derived from user's knowledge, personal experience, or explicit training.

In summary, GOMS describes the procedure or "how-to-do-it" knowledge of how to perform a task by a human user [12].

2.2.2 KLM

Keystroke-level model (KLM) was introduced by Stuart K. Card, Thomas P. Moran and Allen Newell in their work published in 1980 [8]. Based on a serial stage model of human information processing (i.e., processing one action at a time until the goal is accomplished), KLM is different from GOMS. KLM does not have goals, methods, and selection rules, but only keystroke-level operators with a few "mental operator" determined by simple heuristics to model required action events such as keystrokes, mouse movements, mouse-button events. The underlying cognitive architecture of serial stage model and the way to estimate mental operators allow KLM to model tasks that can be approximated by a series of operators, but restrict KLM to model tasks that have parallel sub-tasks, or task with interruptions.

There are six operators for KLM as shown below, where four of them are physical motor operators, and one is mental operator, and another one is system response operator.

- Motor operator **K** represents keystroke or button presses
- Motor operator **P** is the action of pointing to a target on a display with a mouse
- Motor operator **H** represents homing the hand(s) on the device (e.g., keyboard)
- Motor operator **D** is the action of drawing (manually)
- Mental operator **M** means the mental preparation for initiating and executing physical actions
- System response operator **R** corresponds to the response time of the system

Each operator has an estimate of execution time. Similar to the GOMS model, the time could be a constant value, or a parameterized estimate, or a value derived from distribution, or a value derived from a function. In addition, a set of five heuristic rules are also included in KLM [9] for estimating mental preparation time during a task that requires several physical operators [12]. KLM is the underlying psychological theory for the cognitive modeling software tool 'CogTool', which will be introduced in Chap. 3.

2.2.3 CPM-GOMS

CPM stands for **C**ognitive-**P**erceptual-**M**otor. It is also referred as **C**ritical-**P**ath-**M**ethod, as the schedule chart method uses the critical path to make the task time prediction. Similar to other models in the GOMS family, CPM-GOMS predicts execution time. However, unlike other GOMS extended versions, CPM-GOMS supports parallel performance for perceptual, cognitive, and motor operators rather than assuming that operators are performed serially. CPM-GOMS is based on a basic human information processing architecture (MHP [9]). The information is firstly processed in working memory by perceptual processors, and then a cognitive processor commands motor processors to make actions based on the information processed by the perceptual processors [12]. The assumption is that each processor operates serially internally, but they can run in parallel. The schedule chart or PERT chart [10] is used for CPM-GOMS to describe the operators and the dependent relationship between operators. CPM-GOMS is the underlying psychological theory for the cognitive modeling software tool 'SANLab-CM', which will be briefly reviewed in Chap. 3.

2.2.4 Comparison

For unobservable operators, all GOMS variants models make assumptions. Among all, KLM makes the simplest assumption by merging all operations such as perceiving information, decisions, eye movements, and mental calculations into one operator (i.e., M, 1.35 seconds in length). This operator is always placed at the beginning of a cognitive unit. Similarly, CPM-GOMS also utilizes the cycle times of the Model Human Processor (MHP) processors to represent the underlying unobserved operations. The difference is that the dependent relationships between other operators determine the critical path.

In summary, KLM is a model that is easy to apply. However, it can predict execution time using only the methods supplied by the analyst. In comparison with KLM, with analyst-supplied methods, CPM-GOMs can predict execution time in greater details including subtle estimation and overlapping patterns of activities [12].

References

1. Anderson, J.R.: This week's citation classic. Current Contents (52), 91 (1979). http://garfield.library.upenn.edu/classics1979/A1979HX09600001.pdf
2. Anderson, J.R., Bothell, D., Byrne, M.D., Douglass, S., Lebiere, C., Qin, Y.: An integrated theory of the mind. Psychol. Rev. **111**(4), 1036–1060 (2004)
3. Anderson, J.R., Lebiere, C.: The newell test for a theory of cognition. Behav. Brain Sci. **26**(5), 587–601 (2003)
4. Anderson, J.R.J.R.: The Adaptive Character of Thought. Studies in Cognition. L. Erlbaum Associates, Hillsdale (1990)
5. Anderson, J.R.J.R.: How Can the Human Mind Occur in the Physical Universe? Oxford Series on Cognitive Models and Architectures. Oxford University Press, Oxford (2007)
6. Borst, J.P., Anderson, J.R.: A step-by-step tutorial on using the cognitive architecture ACT-R in combination with fmRI data. J. Math. Psychol. **76**, 94–103 (2017)
7. Byrne, M.D., Anderson, J.R.: Serial modules in parallel: the psychological refractory period and perfect time-sharing. Psychol. Rev. **108**(4), 847–869 (2001)
8. Card, S., Moran, T., Newell, A.: The keystroke-level model for user performance time with interactive systems. Commun. ACM **23**(7), 396–410 (1980)
9. Card, S.K., Newell, A., Moran, T.P.: The Psychology of Human-Computer Interaction. L. Erlbaum Associates Inc., USA (1983)
10. Stires, D.M., Murphy, M.M.: PERT (Program Evaluation and Review Technique) CPM (Critical Path Method). Materials Management Inst., Boston (1962)
11. Hélie, S., Sun, R.: Incubation, insight, and creative problem solving: a unified theory and a connectionist model. Psychol. Rev. **117**(3), 994–1024 (2010)
12. John, B.E., Kieras, D.E.: The goms family of user interface analysis techniques: comparison and contrast. ACM Trans. Comput.-Hum. Interact. **3**(4), 320–351 (1996). https://doi.org/10.1145/235833.236054
13. Jones, R.M., Laird, J.E., Nielsen, P.E., Coulter, K.J., Kenny, P., Koss, F.V.: Automated intelligent pilots for combat flight simulation. AI Mag. **20**(1), 27 (1999). https://www.aaai.org/ojs/index.php/aimagazine/article/view/1438
14. Kennedy, W.G., Afb, W.P.: Modeling intuitive decision making in ACT-R (2012)

15. Kieras, D., Marshall, S.P.: Visual availability and fixation memory in modeling visual search using the epic architecture (2006). http://www.escholarship.org/uc/item/8xq582jf
16. Kieras, D.E., Wakefield, G.H., Thompson, E.R., Iyer, N., Simpson, B.D.: Modeling two-channel speech processing with the epic cognitive architecture. Top. Cogn. Sci. **8**(1), 291–304 (2016)
17. Kieras, D.E., Meyer, D.E.: An overview of the epic architecture for cognition and performance with application to human-computer interaction. Hum.-Comput. Interact. **12**(4), 391–438 (1997). https://doi.org/10.1207/s15327051hci1204_4
18. Kotseruba, I., Tsotsos, J.: A review of 40 years of cognitive architecture research: core cognitive abilities and practical applications. arXiv.org (2018). http://search.proquest.com/docview/2071239777/
19. Laird, J.E.: Preface for special section on integrated cognitive architectures. SIGART Bull. **2**(4), 12–13 (1991). https://doi.org/10.1145/122344.1063801
20. Laird, J.E., Lebiere, C., Rosenbloom, P.S.: A standard model of the mind: toward a common computational framework across artificial intelligence, cognitive science, neuroscience, and robotics. AI Mag. **38**(4), 13–26 (2017)
21. Laird, J.E., Newell, A., Rosenbloom, P.S.: Soar: an architecture for general intelligence. Artif. Intell. **33**(1), 1–64 (1987)
22. Laird, J.E.J.L.: Soar Cognitive Architecture. MIT Press, Cambridge (2012)
23. Lebiere, C.: The dynamics of cognition: an ACT-R model of cognitive arithmetic. Kognitionswissenschaft **8**(1), 5–19 (1999). https://doi.org/10.1007/BF03354932
24. Marr, D.: Vision: A Computational Investigation into the Human Representation and Processing of Visual Information. Freeman, New York (1982)
25. Meyer, D.E., Kieras, D.E.: A computational theory of executive cognitive processes and multiple-task performance: Part 1. Basic mechanisms. Psychol. Rev. **104**(1), 3–65 (1997)
26. Möbus, C., Lenk, J.C., Özyurt, J., Thiel, C.M., Claassen, A.: Checking the ACT-R/brain mapping hypothesis with a complex task: using fmRI and Bayesian identification in a multi-dimensional strategy space. Cogn. Syst. Res. **12**(3–4), 321–335 (2011)
27. Newell, A., Simon, H.: GPS, a Program That Simulates Human Thought. McGraw-Hill, New York (1963)
28. Newell, A.: You Can't Play 20 Questions with Nature and Win: Projective Comments on the Papers of This Symposium, pp. 283–308. Academic, New York (1973)
29. Newell, A.: Physical symbol systems. Cogn. Sci. **4**(2), 135–183 (1980)
30. Newell, A.: Unified Theories of Cognition. Harvard University Press, USA (1990)
31. Oh, H., Jo, S., Myung, R.: Computational modeling of human performance in multiple monitor environments with ACT-R cognitive architecture. Int. J. Indus. Ergon. **44**(6), 857–865 (2014)
32. Paik, J., Pirolli, P.: ACT-R models of information foraging in geospatial intelligence tasks (report). Comput. Math. Organ. Theory **21**(3), 274–295 (2015)
33. Ritter, F.E., Baxter, G.D., Jones, G., Young, R.M.: Supporting cognitive models as users. ACM Trans. Comput.-Hum. Interact. **7**(2), 141–173 (2000). https://doi.org/10.1145/353485.353486
34. Ritter, F.E., Tehranchi, F., Oury, J.D.: ACT-R: a cognitive architecture for modeling cognition. WIREs Cogn. Sci. **10**(3), e1488 (2019). https://doi.org/10.1002/wcs.1488
35. Rosenbloom, P.S., Laird, J.E., Newell, A., Mccarl, R.: A preliminary analysis of the soar architecture as a basis for general intelligence. Artif. Intell. **47**(1–3), 289–325 (1991)
36. Rumelhart, D.E., McClelland, J.L.: Parallel Distributed Processing: Explorations in the Microstructure of Cognition. Vol.1, Foundations. Computational Models of Cognition and Perception. MIT Press, Cambridge, MA (1986)
37. Salvucci, D.D.: Modeling driver behavior in a cognitive architecture. Hum. Factors **48**(2), 362–380 (2006). https://search.proquest.com/docview/216466223?accountid=17256, copyright – Copyright Human Factors and Ergonomics Society Summer 2006; Document feature – Illustrations; Equations; Charts; Tables; Graphs; Last updated – 2017-11-09; CODEN – HUFAA6
38. Salvucci, D.D.: Rapid prototyping and evaluation of in-vehicle interfaces. ACM Trans. Comput.-Hum. Interact. **16**(2) (2009). https://doi.org/10.1145/1534903.1534906

39. Salvucci, D.D., Lee, F.J.: Simple cognitive modeling in a complex cognitive architecture. In: Human Factors in Computing Systems: CHI 2003 Conference Proceedings, pp. 265–272. ACM Press (2003)
40. Sun, R., Hélie, S.: Psychologically realistic cognitive agents: taking human cognition seriously. J. Exp. Theor. Artif. Intell. **25**(1), 65–92 (2013). https://doi.org/10.1080/0952813X.2012.661236
41. Sun, R., Merrill, E., Peterson, T.: From implicit skills to explicit knowledge: a bottom-up model of skill learning. Cogn. Sci. **25**(2), 203–244 (2001)
42. Sun, R., Zhang, X.: Accounting for a variety of reasoning data within a cognitive architecture. J. Exp. Theor. Artif. Intell. **18**(2), 169–191 (2006). https://doi.org/10.1080/09528130600557713
43. Taatgen, N., Anderson, J.R.: The past, present, and future of cognitive architectures. Top. Cogn. Sci. **2**(4), 693–704 (2010). https://doi.org/10.1111/j.1756-8765.2009.01063.x
44. Wiiliams, N., Li, S.: Simulating human detection of phishing websites: an investigation into the applicability of ACT-R cognitive behaviour architecture model (2017)
45. Zhang, Z., Russwinkel, N., Prezenski, S.: Modeling individual strategies in dynamic decision-making with ACT-R: a task toward decision-making assistance in HCI. Proc. Comput. Sci. **145**, 668–674 (2018)

Chapter 3
Review of Cognitive Modeling Software Tools

Abstract A large number of cognitive models have been developed and widely used in the HCI domain. GOMS (Gray et al (1993) Hum Comput Interact 8(3):237–309; John and Kieras (1996) ACM Trans Comput-Hum Interact 3(4):320–351) is one of the well-established models for predicting human performance and facilitating UI design. As mentioned in Chap. 2, a number of variants of GOMS models such as KLM (Card et al (1980) Commun ACM 23(7):396–410) and CPM-GOMS (John and Kieras (1996) ACM Trans Comput-Hum Interact 3(4):320–351) are useful to predict task completion time, and to refine UI designs and human task procedures (Paik et al (2015) ACM Trans Comput-Hum Interact 22(5):25:1–25:26. https://doi.org/10.1145/2776891). In this chapter, we present a review of existing software tools that materializing these cognitive models so that they can be used by people without advanced knowledge on cognitive modelling. Although there are lots of existing tools, we mainly introduce CogTool, SANLab-CM, and Cogulator in this chapter. The main reason is that they are well maintained open source projects with a considerable size of user base. In addition, this chapter lists some examples of applying cognitive models and relevant software tools in both HCI and cyber security domains. Furthermore, this chapter concludes with a discussion on issues and challenges of using existing software tools to model complex systems.

3.1 Cognitive Modeling Simulation Software

3.1.1 CogTool

CogTool was developed at the Carnegie-Mellon University in the USA. It is an open source software tool[1] for UI prototyping that utilizes human performance models (i.e., KLM model implemented using the ACT-R cognitive architecture [1, 2]) to

[1] Available at https://github.com/cogtool/cogtool

H. Yuan et al., *Cognitive Modeling for Automated Human Performance Evaluation at Scale*, Human–Computer Interaction Series,
https://doi.org/10.1007/978-3-030-45704-4_3

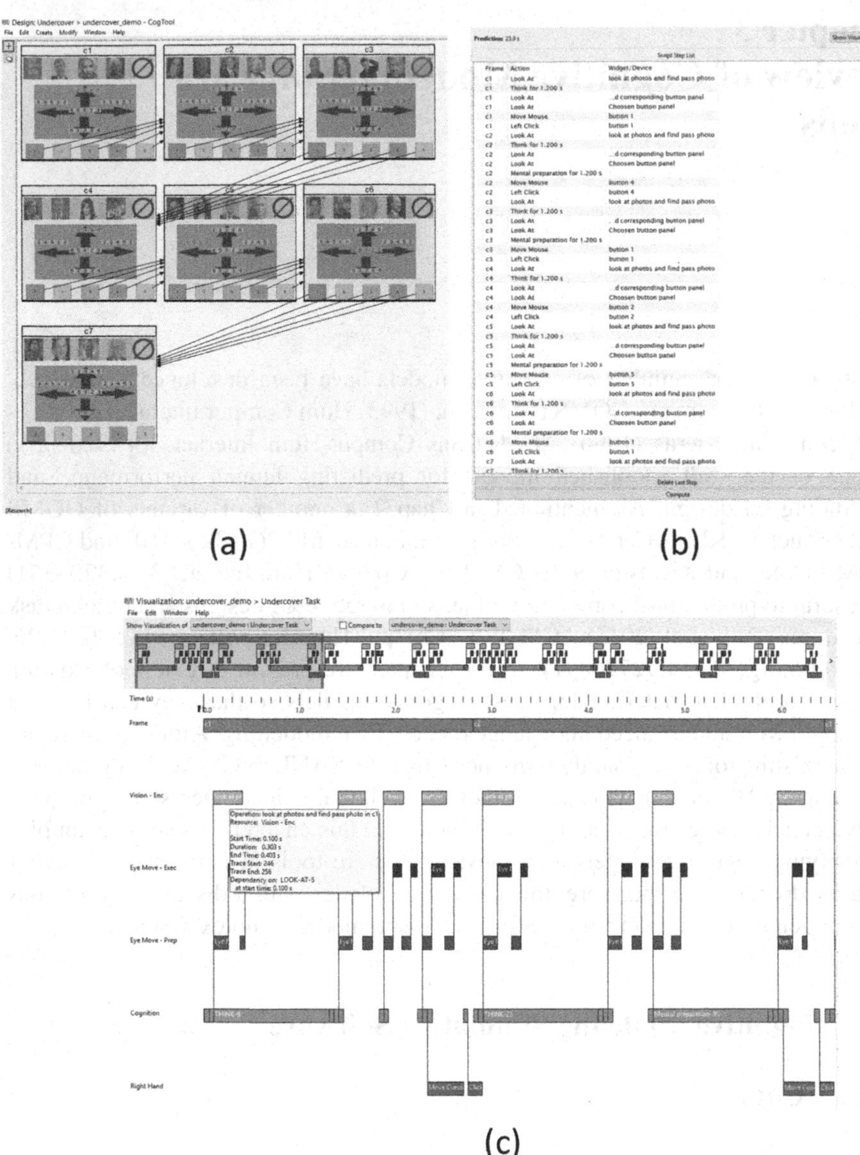

Fig. 3.1 Screenshots of using CogTool GUI to model 'Undercover' system [25]: (**a**) CogTool design interface (**b**) CogTool trace prediction interface (**c**) CogTool results visualisation interface

simulate the cognitive, perceptual, and motor behaviors of humans, and predict execution time by skilled users to complete computer tasks [15].

The dedicated graphical user interface (GUI) of CogTool makes it easier for researchers and designers to create a storyboard of a design idea with sketches, images or on a canvas with CogTool's widgets (see Fig. 3.1 for some examples).

The psychological theory (i.e., KLM version of human information processing (HIP) theory) underlying CogTool has been used and validated by the HCI research community and industry users over the decades [13]. It is specific to skilled human behaviors around computer-based tasks with certain time parameters [13], and it consists of three modules:

- A **perception module** takes information from the world and passes it to a cognitive module. In CogTool, the perception takes around 100 ms, as it is relatively easy to perceive signals in computer-based tasks compared with conditions like extremely low light for visual signals or high noise for auditory signals.
- A **cognitive module** processes the information from the perception model. Then the processed information could combine with information from other sources such as long-term memory to send commands to a motor module. Here, a mental operator (M) represents a combination of all un-observable activities, including cognitive and perceptual activities such as comprehending perceptual input and recognising the situation, command recall, and decisions. Card, Moran, and Newell empirically estimated M to be 1,350 ms [15]. In CogTool, M is estimated to be 1,200 ms by default to accommodate the ACT-R architecture, which normally requires a 150 ms look-at operator to accompany each typical mental operation.
- A **motor module** manipulates the prototype to take action in the world. The motor module in KLM for desktop applications includes operators for pressing keys (K), pointing (P), and homing between the keyboard and the mouse. The execution time of the motor operator is based on the psychology literature, where K depends on typing speed, and P is determined by the target's size and distance moved of Fitts's Law [9].

In addition, researchers have been working on developing extended versions of CogTool to support automation and other advanced features. Working with existing OpenOffice application or Java Swing application, CogTool-Helper [28] can automatically create frames with no human intervention. Human performance regression testing (HPRT) is developed based on the CogTool-Helper [29]. With certain knowledge of using CogTool and a GUI Testing frAmeworRk (GUITAR) [20], users can utilize HPRT's capability to generate all possible interaction paths and perform human performance predictions. Furthermore, researchers have built other software tools on the basis of CogTool. For instance, Feuerstack and Wortelen [8] adopted the front end of CogTool to develop the Human Efficiency Evaluator (HEE), which is used to make predictions for attention distribution and average reaction time.

3.1.2 SANLab-CM

The Stochastic Activity Network Laboratory for Cognitive Modeling (SANLab-CM) was developed at the Rensselaer Polytechnic Instituteis [23]. It is an open source software tool[2] that is specialized to rapidly create CPM-GOMS models in order to predict how humans interact with external systems and build models of existing human data as a measure of validity checking.[3] Compared with other CPM-GOMS modeling tools, SANLab-CM can add variability to its modeling tasks. This leads to new challenges and opportunities. The variation of operator execution times can cause a wide fluctuation of the critical paths that can affect the task completion prediction. Hence, SANLab-CM has a set of tools developed to facilitate visualization and comparison of critical paths (see Fig. 3.2) to provide better ways to investigating differences between critical paths.

Compared with CogTool, SANLab-CM can model parallel processes and output results in a distribution format. A study of comparing SANLab-CM with CogTool for entering the landing speed into the Boeing 777 Flight Management Computer using the Control and Display Unit [16] revealed that the distribution produced by SANLab-CM only represents the individual differences within a method, and it does not represent different methods for accomplishing a task. For example, it does not predict the time differences using menu vs. keyboard shortcuts, but the variation in human behavior (i.e., completion time) when using either the menu or the keyboard shortcuts. The study also suggests that it would be useful to design multiple design methods using CogTool, and import these CogTool projects to SANLab-CM to make predictions of time distributions that can represent both individual differences as well as methodological differences.

3.1.3 Cogulator

Inspired by GLEAN,[4] Cogulator was designed and developed to be a simple human performance modeling tool for estimating task time, working memory load, and mental workload.[5] There are a number of features that distinguish Cogulator from other existing modeling tools [7]:

1. Most modeling tools require changes to the code base in order to add new operators or change operator's execution time. Differently, Cogulator allows the user to add new operators and/or change execution time without changing the application's source code.
2. Different from other modeling tools, Cogulator supports building multiple GOMS-based models such as KLM, NGOMSL [17], CPM-GOMS [11], CMN-GOMS [6]. An user can choose any one of the above models when starting a Cogulator project.

---

[2] Available at https://github.com/CogWorks/SANLab-CM

[3] http://cogworks.cogsci.rpi.edu/projects/software/sanlab-cm/

[4] https://web.eecs.umich.edu/~kieras/goms.html

[5] http://cogulator.io/primer.html

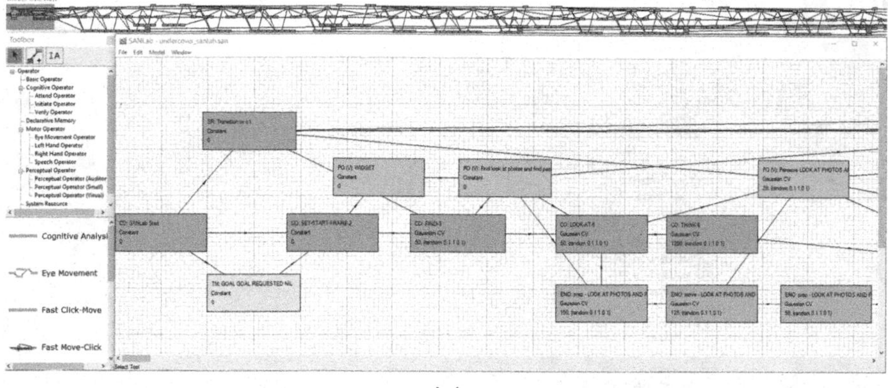

(a)

(b)

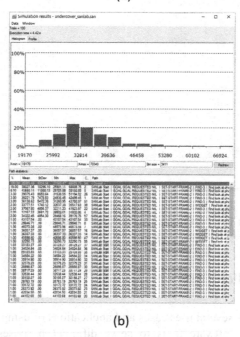

Fig. 3.2 Screenshots of using SANLab-CM to model 'Undercover' system [25]: (**a**) Visualization of critical paths, (**b**) distribution of prediction times

3. Cogulator features a text-based interface for the user to build models (see Fig. 3.3 for some examples).

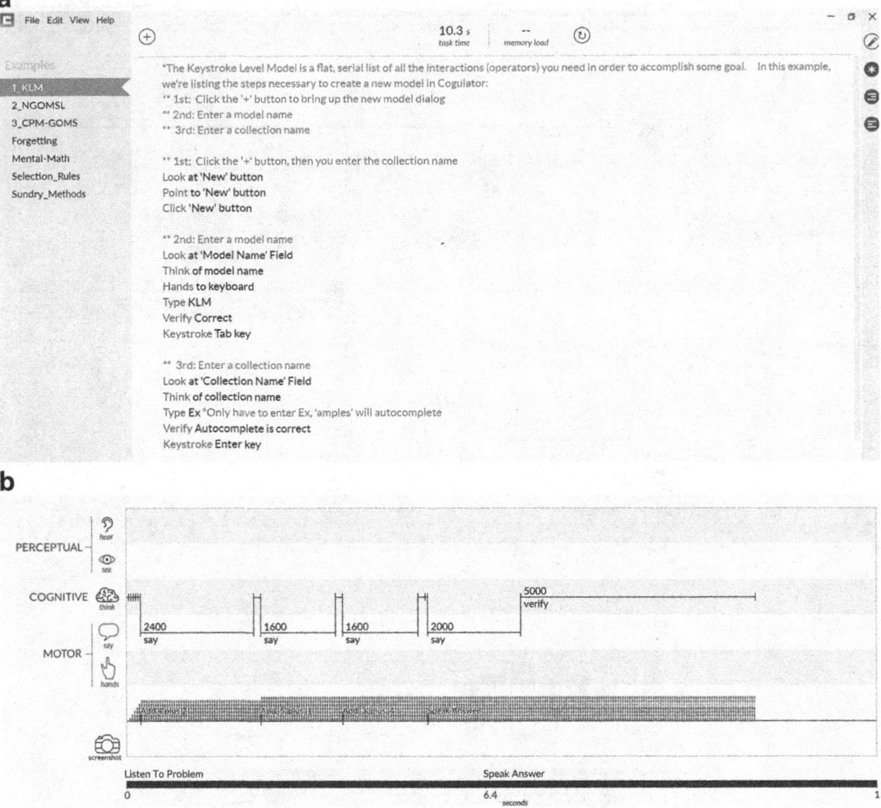

Fig. 3.3 Screenshots of using Cogulator: (**a**) Text-based interface with choice of KLM, CPM-GOMS, and NGMOSL (**b**) Interface for visualising predictions and memory load

3.2 Cases Studies

This section presents several uses cases and applications of using above-introduced cognitive modeling software tools to serve different purposes such as human performance evaluation, UI design, and UI refinement, for both HCI and cyber security systems/tasks.

CogTool has proven to be a useful and popular tool in various research areas, and thereby has a relatively large size of user base. In a study of investigating hand-held devices, Luo and John [19] demonstrated that the prediction time estimated by CogTool can match the execution time obtained from actual human user studies. Teo and John [30] used CogTool to model and evaluate a web-based experiment. The results suggested that CogTool can make better predictions than other existing tools. More recently, Gartenberg et al. [10] evaluated a mobile health application with two UI designs using CogTool. They revealed that the simulated user performance is consistent with the findings obtained from a user study involving real human participants.

Apart from academic research, CogTool has been applied in industrial applications. CogTool is used to evaluate the usability of a new parallel programming Eclipse toolkit by comparing with a command line programming interface [3]. Although programmers preferred command line interface, the data suggested that the mouse-based programming is faster than the keyboard-based command line interface. Researchers from IBM and Carnegie Mellon University [4] integrated CogTool into software development teams, aiming to improve the usability analysis and communication within a team, as well as between a team and its customers. Furthermore, by comparing CogTool simulation time with actual completion time obtained from lab studies for an industrial application in an agile environment, researchers [27] revealed a positive correlation between the two.

Both CogTool and SANLab-CM were used to evaluate tasks of entering the landing speed into the Boeing 777 Flight Management Computer [16]. Researchers also used SANLab-CM to explore the impact of the age on the predictive models of human performance [31]. Researchers modeled and explored a single pilot's thoughts and actions during the approaching phase of flight using Cogulator to work out the pilot's task times, heads down times, and working memory load [32].

Apart from being used for HCI research related topics, cognitive modeling tools have been used for more applied research areas such as cyber security research. For instance, CogTool was used to evaluate a shoulder surfing resistant mobile user authentication system [18], and it was used in combination with a real human user study to evaluate the usability of another user authentication system [26]. In addition, authors of the book also combined the eye tracking data and CogTool to model a user authentication system [33]. We discovered that the simulated data can reveal the same human-related security issues and UI design flaws that had been identified in a previous user study [24].

3.3 Issues and Challenges

Among the three above-introduced modeling tools, CogTool has the largest user base. However, CogTool has some limitations inherited from the GOMS-type models despite its popularity. In CogTool, there is no support to estimate the time related to the learning processes [22], meaning that CogTool cannot predict the time needed for a novice user to become a skilled user. This information could be valuable for UI/UX design and evaluation. Shankar et al. [27] suggested that the default value of 'thinking time' in CogTool is under-estimated compared with the actual value of 'thinking time' in some specific cases. The CogTool research community be noticed this issue, and CogTool now has the capability to allow the user to change the value of such variables manually. Similarly, Cogulator also allows users to change execution time of operators manually. Nevertheless, Ocak and Cagiltay [21] argued that the execution time of operators should be modified dynamically depending on the context of use. To be more specific, they indicated that the execution time for the 'Look-at' operator in CogTool should be set automatically based on the length of the text in a reading scenario. Furthermore, our previous work [33] identified that there is a need to interface CogTool with external data to better tailor the modeling tasks.

References

1. ACT-R Research Group: ACT-R. http://act-r.psy.cmu.edu/ (2016). Accessed: 25 Aug 2016
2. Anderson, J.: How Can the Human Mind Occur in the Physical Universe? Oxford University Press, Oxford (2007)
3. Bellamy, R., John, B., Richards, J., Thomas, J.: Using cogtool to model programming tasks. In: Evaluation and Usability of Programming Languages and Tool, PLATEAU'10, pp. 1:1–1:6. ACM, New York (2010). https://doi.org/10.1145/1937117.1937118
4. Bellamy, R., John, B., Kogan, S.: Deploying CogTool: integrating quantitative usability assessment into real-world software development. In: Proceedings of 2011 33rd International Conference on Software Engineering (ICSE 2011), pp. 691–700. IEEE, Honolulu (2011)
5. Card, S., Moran, T., Newell, A.: The keystroke-level model for user performance time with interactive systems. Commun. ACM **23**(7), 396–410 (1980)
6. Card, S.K., Newell, A., Moran, T.P.: The Psychology of Human-Computer Interaction. L. Erlbaum Associates Inc., USA (1983)
7. Estes, S.: Introduction to simple workload models using cogulator (01 2016)
8. Feuerstack, S., Wortelen, B.: Revealing differences in designers' and users' perspectives. In: Abascal, J., Barbosa, S., Fetter, M., Gross, T., Palanque, P., Winckler, M. (eds.) Human-Computer Interaction – INTERACT 2015, pp. 105–122. Springer International Publishing, Cham (2015)
9. Fitts, P.: The information capacity of the human motor system in controlling the amplitude of movement. J. Exp. Psychol. **47**(6), 381–391 (1954)
10. Gartenberg, D., Thornton, R., Masood, M., Pfannenstiel, D., Taylor, D., Parasuraman, R.: Collecting health-related data on the smart phone: mental models, cost of collection, and perceived benefit of feedback. Pers. Ubiquit. Comput. **17**(3), 561–570 (2013)
11. Gray, W.D., John, B.E., Atwood, M.E.: The precis of project ernestine or an overview of a validation of goms. In: Proceedings of the SIGCHI Conference on Human Factors in Computing Systems, CHI'92, pp. 307–312. Association for Computing Machinery, New York (1992). https://doi.org/10.1145/142750.142821
12. Gray, W.D., John, B.E., Atwood, M.E.: Project Ernestine: validating a GOMS analysis for predicting and explaining real-world task performance. Hum. Comput. Interact. **8**(3), 237–309 (1993)
13. John, B.E., Salvucci, D.D.: Multipurpose prototypes for assessing user interfaces in pervasive computing systems. IEEE Pervasive Comput. **4**(4), 27–34 (2005)
14. John, B., Kieras, D.: The GOMS family of user interface analysis techniques: comparison and contrast. ACM Trans. Comput.-Hum. Interact. **3**(4), 320–351 (1996)
15. John, B., Prevas, K., Salvucci, D., Koedinger, K.: Predictive human performance modeling made easy. In: Proceedings of the SIGCHI Conference on Human Factors in Computing Systems, CHI'04, pp. 455–462. ACM, New York (2004). https://doi.org/10.1145/985692.985750
16. John, B.E., Patton, E.W., Gray, W.D., Morrison, D.F.: Tools for predicting the duration and variability of skilled: performance without skilled performers. Proc. Hum. Factors Ergon. Soc. Annu. Meet. **56**(1), 985–989 (2012). https://doi.org/10.1177/1071181312561206

17. Kieras, D.E.: Towards a practical goms model methodology for user interface design, Chapter 7. In: Helander, M. (ed.) Handbook of Human-Computer Interaction, pp. 135–157. North-Holland, Amsterdam (1988). http://www.sciencedirect.com/science/article/pii/B9780444705365500129
18. Kim, S., Yi, H., Yi, J.: Fakepin: dummy key based mobile user authentication scheme. In: Ubiquitous Information Technologies and Applications, pp. 157–164. Springer, Berlin/Heidelberg (2014)
19. Luo, L., John, B.: Predicting task execution time on handheld devices using the keystroke-level model. In: CHI'05 Extended Abstracts on Human Factors in Computing Systems, CHI EA'05, pp. 1605–1608. ACM, New York (2005). https://doi.org/10.1145/1056808.1056977
20. Nguyen, B.N., Robbins, B., Banerjee, I., Memon, A.: Guitar: an innovative tool for automated testing of gui-driven software. Autom. Softw. Eng. **21**(1), 65–105 (2014). https://doi.org/10.1007/s10515-013-0128-9
21. Ocak, N., Cagiltay, K.: Comparison of cognitive modeling and user performance analysis for touch screen mobile interface design. Int. J. Hum.-Comput. Interact. **33**(8), 633–641 (2017)
22. Paik, J., Kim, J., Ritter, F., Reitter, D.: Predicting user performance and learning in human–computer interaction with the herbal compiler. ACM Trans. Comput.-Hum. Interact. **22**(5), 25:1–25:26 (2015). https://doi.org/10.1145/2776891
23. Patton, E., Gray, W.: SANLab-CM: a tool for incorporating stochastic operations into activity network modeling. Behav. Res. Methods **42**, 877–83 (2010)
24. Perković, T., Li, S., Mumtaz, A., Khayam, S., Javed, Y., Čagalj, M.: Breaking undercover: exploiting design flaws and nonuniform human behavior. In: Proceedings of the Seventh Symposium on Usable Privacy and Security, SOUPS'11, pp. 5:1–5:15. ACM, New York (2011). https://doi.org/10.1145/2078827.2078834
25. Sasamoto, H., Christin, N., Hayashi, E.: Undercover: authentication usable in front of prying eyes. In: Proceedings of the SIGCHI Conference on Human Factors in Computing Systems, CHI'08, pp. 183–192. ACM, New York (2008). https://doi.org/10.1145/1357054.1357085
26. Sasse, M., Steves, M., Krol, K., Chisnell, D.: The great authentication fatigue – and how to overcome it. In: Rau, P.L.P. (ed.) Cross-Cultural Design, pp. 228–239. Springer International Publishing, Cham (2014)
27. Shankar, A., Lin, H., Brown, H., Rice, C.: Rapid usability assessment of an enterprise application in an agile environment with cogtool. In: Proceedings of the 33rd Annual ACM Conference Extended Abstracts on Human Factors in Computing Systems, CHI EA'15, pp. 719–726. ACM, New York (2015). https://doi.org/10.1145/2702613.2702960
28. Swearngin, A., Cohen, M., John, B., Bellamy, R.: Easing the generation of predictive human performance models from legacy systems. In: Proceedings of the SIGCHI Conference on Human Factors in Computing Systems, CHI'12, pp. 2489–2498. ACM, New York (2012). https://doi.org/10.1145/2207676.2208415
29. Swearngin, A., Cohen, M.B., John, B.E., Bellamy, R.K.E.: Human performance regression testing. In: Proceedings of the 2013 International Conference on Software Engineering, ICSE'13, pp. 152–161. IEEE Press, Piscataway (2013). http://dl.acm.org/citation.cfm?id=2486788.2486809
30. Teo, L., John, B.: Cogtool-explorer: towards a tool for predicting user interaction. In: CHI'08 Extended Abstracts on Human Factors in Computing Systems, CHI EA'08, pp. 2793–2798. ACM, New York (2008). https://doi.org/10.1145/1358628.1358763
31. Trewin, S., John, B., Richards, J., Sloan, D., Hanson, V., Bellamy, R., Thomas, J., Swart, C.: Age-specific predictive models of human performance. In: CHI'12 Extended Abstracts on Human Factors in Computing Systems, CHI EA'12, pp. 2267–2272. Association for Computing Machinery, New York (2012). https://doi.org/10.1145/2212776.2223787

32. Wilkins, S.A.: Examination of pilot benefits from cognitive assistance for single-pilot general aviation operations. In: 2017 IEEE/AIAA 36th Digital Avionics Systems Conference (DASC), pp. 1–9 (2017)
33. Yuan, H., Li, S., Rusconi, P., Aljaffan, N.: When eye-tracking meets cognitive modeling: applications to cyber security systems. In: Human Aspects of Information Security, Privacy and Trust: 5th International Conference, HAS 2017, Held as Part of HCI International 2017, Vancouver, 9–14 July 2017, Proceedings. Lecture Notes in Computer Science, vol. 10292, pp. 251–264. Springer, Cham (2017)

Chapter 4
Integration of Behavioral Data

Abstract As demonstrated in previous chapters, human cognitive modeling techniques and related software tools have been widely used by researchers and practitioners to evaluate user interface (UI) designs and related human performance. However, for a system involving a relatively complicated UI, it could be difficult to build a cognitive model that accurately captures the different cognitive tasks involved in all user interactions.

The integration of human behavioral data could be useful to help the cognitive modeling process. This chapter firstly provides an overview of how behavioral data, particularly eye tracking data, can be used in cognitive modeling, followed by presenting two user studies of incorporating human behavior/data in the process of creating human cognitive models to better estimate human performance and evaluate UI (part of this chapter previously appeared in Yuan et al. (When eye-tracking meets cognitive modeling: applications to cyber security systems. In: Human Aspects of Information Security, Privacy and Trust: 5th International Conference, HAS 2017, Held as Part of HCI International 2017, Vancouver, 9–14 July 2017, Proceedings. Lecture notes in computer science, vol. 10292, pp 251–264. Springer, Cham (2017))).

4.1 Using Human Behavioral Data in Cognitive Modeling

Eye-tracking data can reveal human users' eye movements such as fixations and saccades, as well as revealing scan paths and other metrics such as pupil dilation and blink rates. These data could provide information about a person's cognitive processes while performing a task, and thereby they have been widely used in studies on cognitive modeling especially on cognitive tasks related to visual objects shown on computer displays [12].

In addition, eye-tracking data has also been used in studies to help validate and compare cognitive models of visual search tasks [4, 8, 13, 23]. Moreover, security researchers utilised eye-tracking data to better understand human users' cognitive processes when interacting with security-sensitive systems: recently Miyamoto et

H. Yuan et al., *Cognitive Modeling for Automated Human Performance Evaluation at Scale*, Human–Computer Interaction Series,
https://doi.org/10.1007/978-3-030-45704-4_4

al. [19] conducted a study on using eye-tracking data to investigate the impact of UI elements on the detection of possible phishing websites; Alsharnouby et al. [1] used eye trackers to assess the influence of browser security indicators and the awareness of phishing on a user's ability to avoid cyber attacks.

4.2 Case Studies: Using an Eye Tracker to Model a Cyber Security System

In this section, we present our work on integrating eye-tracking behavior data with CogTool [14], a widely-used cognitive modeling tool, to model human cognitive tasks of using a relatively complex user authentication system named as 'Undercover [24]'. We demonstrate that the eye-tracking data can be utilized to facilitate the modeling process, and helped to reproduce some *non-uniform* and *insecure* human behavior observed in a previous lab-based user study reported by Perković et al. [21]. In addition, the simulation results produced by the eye-tracking assisted cognitive model led to more insights to offer possible explanations of the observed non-uniform human behavior, and informed us how the UI design may be further refined to improve its security, going beyond what Perković et al. predicted in [21]. This case study suggests that cyber security researchers and practitioners could benefit from a *combined* use of cognitive modeling techniques and eye-tracking data.

4.2.1 Eye-Tracking Assisted Cognitive Modeling Experiment

This section starts with a brief description of the target system Undercover, followed by presenting details of constructing an initial cognitive models of Undercover to produce simulation results when eye-tracking data were not used. Later in this section, an eye-tracking experiment of observing how users visually interact with the Undercover system is presented, followed by introducing a re-modeling work with new insights emerged from the eye-tracking data.

4.2.2 Target System: Undercover

Undercover [24] is an observer-resistant password system (ORPS) developed based on the concept of partially-observable challenges. A user needs to set the password P "pass-pictures", which is a set of five secret pictures, out of an image pool. For completing an authentication session, the user needs to successfully respond to seven challenge screens, where each challenge screen contains a hidden challenge

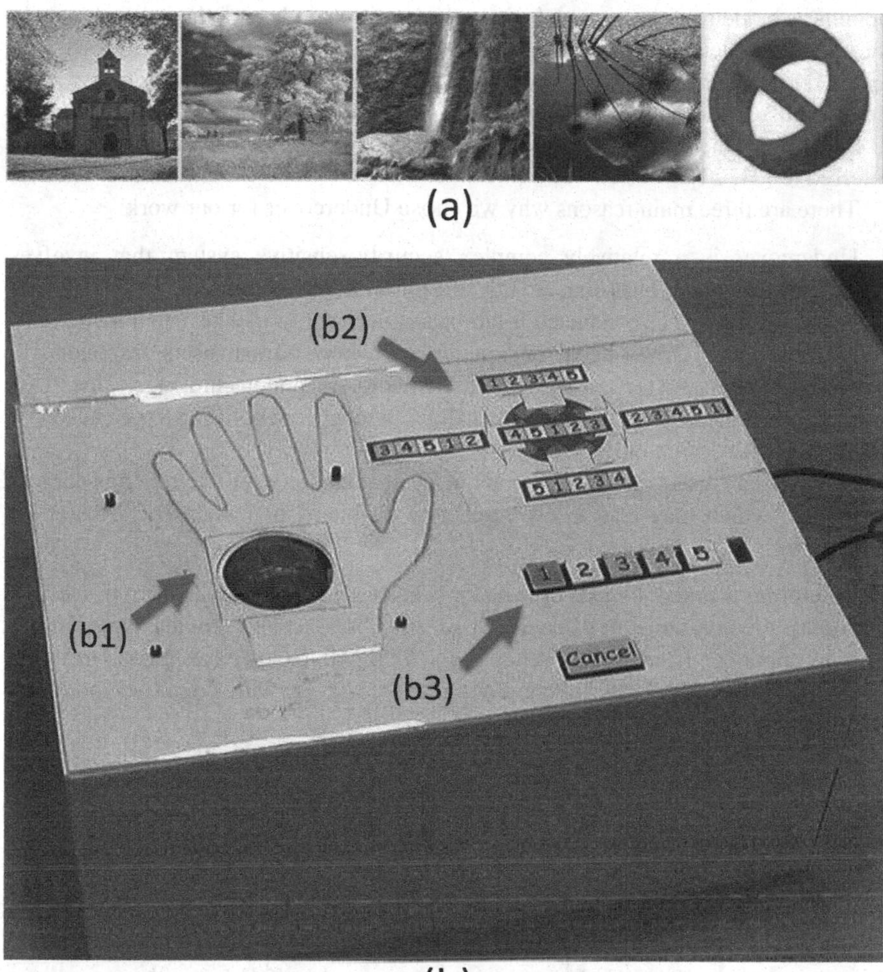

Fig. 4.1 The UI of Undercover [24]: (**a**) the public challenge panel shown on the computer display; (**b**) a box composed of the following UI components: (b1) a track ball for transmitting the hidden challenge, (b2) the hidden challenge button layout panel, (b3) the response button panel

c_h described below and a public challenge c_p consists of four pictures and a "no pass-picture" icon as shown in Fig. 4.1a. The hidden challenge c_h is transmitted via a haptic device (a track ball) covered by the user's palm, as shown in Fig. 4.1b1. Five different rotation/vibration modes of the track ball correspond to five different values of c_h: "Up", "Down", "Left", "Right", "Center" (vibrating). As illustrated in Fig. 4.1b2, each hidden challenge value corresponds to a specific layout of five response buttons labeled with 1–5. To respond to a challenge screen, the user firstly obtains a hidden response r_h which is the position index of the pass-picture in the public challenge (1–4 if present and 5 if absent). Then the user looks for r_h in the correct hidden challenge button layout to get a new position index r'_h, and finally presses the button labeled with r'_h in the response button panel as shown in Fig. 4.1b3. There are some more subtle security settings, for which readers are referred to [21, 24].

There are three main reasons why we chose Undercover for our work:

1. Undercover is a relatively complex security-sensitive system that involves different cognitive tasks that are not straightforward to model.
2. Perković et al. [21] conducted a lab-based user study that revealed some *non-uniform* and *insecure* behavioral patterns on how human users responded to hidden challenges (the average response time to the hidden challenge value "Up" is significantly smaller than to other values) which were believed to be caused by an improper design of the UI.
3. How human users actually interact with the Undercover UI remains largely unclear which may lead to other security problems or insights of a better UI design.

We therefore wanted to use eye-tracking data and CogTool to see if we can reproduce the non-uniform behavioral patterns observed and provide some further insights about the actual human behaviors, which will then serve as a good example showcasing the usefulness of combining eye tracking with cognitive modeling techniques.

4.2.3 Initial CogTool Models (Without Eye-Tracking Data)

To make an adequate comparison with findings reported by Perković et al. [21], we used CogTool to model their Undercover implementation (which is conceptually the same as the original Undercover system reported in [24] but with some minor changes to the UI and the use of an earphone and an audio channel to transmit the hidden challenge instead). The layout of the UI with functionality of each component (which is called the design script in CogTool), and how humans interact with the UI (which is called the demonstration script in CogTool) are essential to CogTool. Undercover has a static UI layout, but the user interaction is dynamic where different hidden challenges can result in different visual scan paths, and require different buttons to be pressed.

A key problem we met in the modeling task is how to model human users' visual scan paths for the three separate parts of a challenge screen: the public challenge picture panel, the hidden challenge button layout panel, and the response button panel. Since we did not have any clue about the actual visual scan paths, we decided

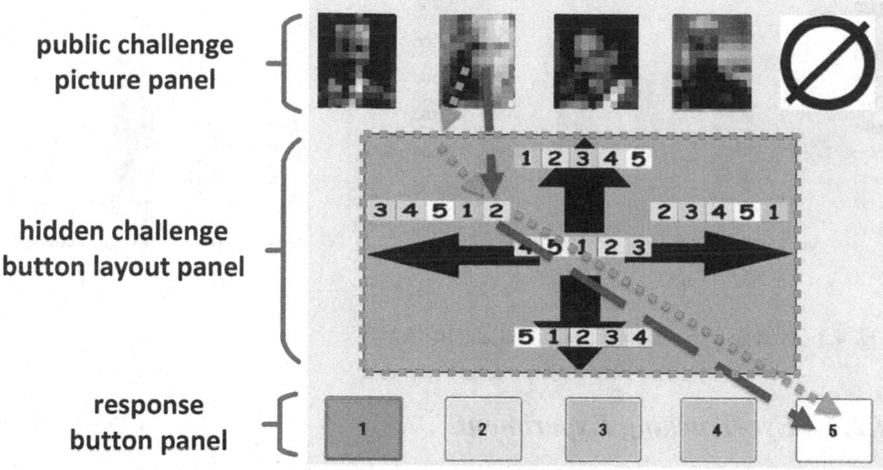

Fig. 4.2 An illustration of the two visual scan paths when the pass-picture is the second picture in the public challenge and the hidden challenge is "Left": the red dashed and dark green dotted lines show **A1** and **A2**, respectively

to make two initial models based on two simple visual scan paths explained below and shown in Fig. 4.2.[1]

- **A1**: for each part of the challenge screen the user identifies the target without an obvious visual searching process, i.e., the user looks at the pass-picture in the public challenge panel, then moves to the (correct) hidden challenge button layout directly, and finally to the (correct) response button directly.
- **A2**: the same as **A1** but before the user looks at the (correct) hidden challenge button layout (s)he looks at the whole hidden challenge button layout panel first.

With the two models, we generated all five possible instances according to the hidden response $r_h = 1, \cdots, 5$ and obtained the average response times as shown in Fig. 4.3.

Comparing the results of **A1** and **A2**, we can see **A2** requires more time due to the added cognitive task, and the hidden challenge value corresponding to the fast average response time differs ("Up" for **A1** and "Center" for **A2**). While the non-uniform response time pattern of **A1** loosely matches the findings reported in [21], the cognitive model is obviously too simplistic, e.g., a proper visual searching process is expected for finding out if a pass-picture is present and where the pass-picture is in the public challenge.

[1]We actually built a number of models for each of the two models as CogTool supports only static cognitive tasks but Undercover involves dynamic ones related to varying challenges. We are developing an extension of CogTool to facilitate modeling of such dynamic cognitive tasks, but in this chapter we will not focus on this issue.

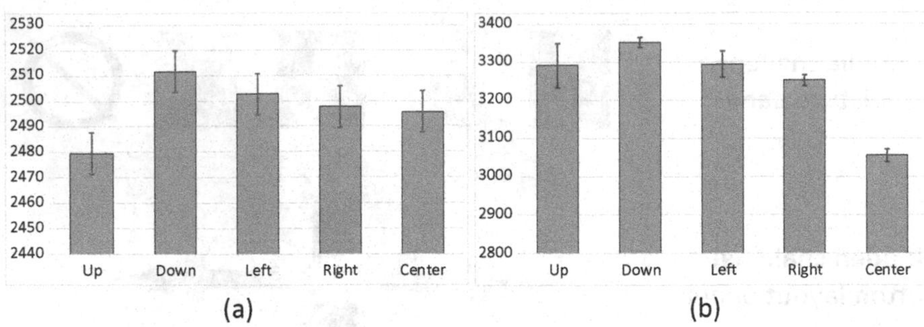

Fig. 4.3 Average response times for (**a**) A1 and (**b**) A2

4.2.4 Eye-Tracking Experiment

As shown above, the lack of knowledge on human users' actual visual scan paths prevented us from making a more informed decision on how to model Undercover. We therefore decided to conduct an eye-tracking experiment in order to gain such knowledge. We implemented a fast prototype of Undercover in MATLAB and used a Tobii EyeX eye tracker (with an upgraded license for research purposes) [30] for the experiment. Nine participants (5 female and 4 male), who did not wear glasses were recruited. Each participant was briefed about Undercover and had a training session to get familiar with the authentication process. We set the same password for all participants, and each participant was given time to memorize the pass-pictures before the actual experiment started.

During the experiment, each participant was asked to complete seven challenge screens (equivalent to one authentication session) once or twice. Among the seven challenge screens, each of the five values of the hidden challenge and the hidden response was present at least once. In total, we collected 98 sets of eye-tracking data (each set represents the process of responding to one challenge screen). We removed 12 sets of data due to inaccuracy caused by change of sitting position during the experiment and incomplete tasks. This gave us 86 valid sets of data whose eye-gaze trajectories were manually inspected to identify visual scan patterns. The results revealed four important (not all expected) visual scan patterns explained below and illustrated in Fig. 4.4.

1. *No obvious searching process for the correct hidden challenge button layout or the correct response button*: For these two parts of the challenge screen, participants identified the targets directly without an obvious visual searching process.
2. *Two searching patterns for the pass-picture*: For 87% cases, participants adopted a searching strategy of center-left-right as illustrated in Fig. 4.4a, and for the rest 13% cases, participants searched for the pass-picture simply from left to right.
3. *Confirmation pattern for the pass-picture*: For 59% of all cases, participants showed a confirmation pattern where they went from the hidden challenge button

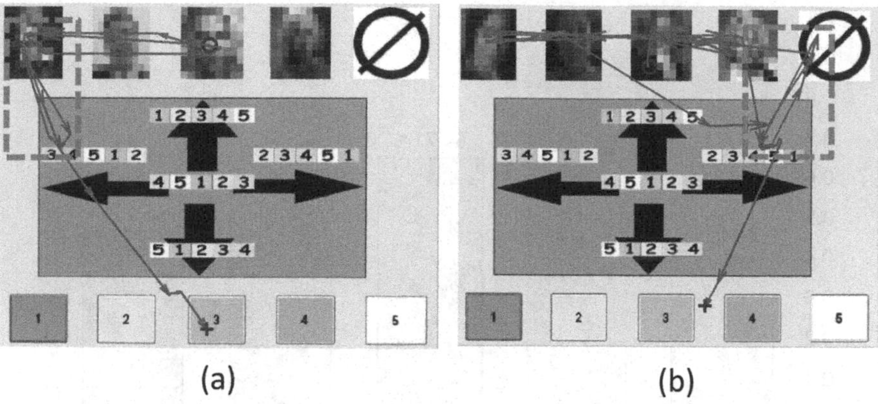

Fig. 4.4 An illustration of observed visual scan patterns where red lines show the eye gaze trajectories, blue circles and blue crosses indicate the starting and ending gazing positions: (**a**) $r_h = 1, c_h =$ Left; (**b**) $r_h = 5, c_h =$ Right

layout panel back to the pass-picture in the public challenge panel before moving to the response button panel, which are highlighted inside the green dash-line rectangles shown in Fig. 4.4. This pattern is consistent with the findings reported in [23], which suggests that several saccades to the location of the memorized target are typical. We also noticed that the confirmation process rate varies depending on the value of the hidden challenge (see Fig. 4.5) c_h: 40.91% (Up), 92.31% (Down), 64.71% (Left), 61.9% (Right), 46.15% (Center). Interestingly, the non-uniform confirmation rates partly match the non-uniform response time reported in [21], suggesting they may be one source of the non-uniformity.

4. *Double scanning pattern for absent pass-picture*: When no pass-picture is present in the public challenge, in 66% cases participants double scanned the public challenge picture panel to make sure there was indeed no pass-picture, which is illustrated in Fig. 4.4b.

4.2.5 Re-modeling Undercover (with Eye-Tracking Data)

The four visual scan path patterns learned from our eye-tracking experiment provided additional evidence for us to remodel Undercover in a more complicated (and hopefully more accurate) manner. We firstly constructed four new models named as CLR-C, CLR-NC, LR-C and LR-NC, where CLR represents the (C)enter-(L)eft-(R)ight searching strategy for the pass-picture; LR represents the simpler (L)eft-(R)ight searching strategy for the pass-picture; C after the hyphen stands for the (C)onfirmation process and NC after the hyphen means there is (N)o (C)onfirmation process. As in the case of the two initial models, for each of the

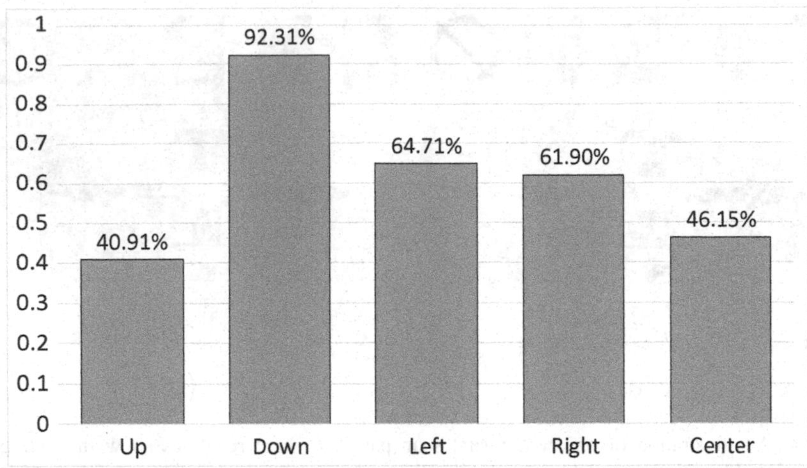

Fig. 4.5 Confirmation rate for hidden challenges

Table 4.1 Average response time (in milliseconds) to each hidden challenge value for different models

Model	Hidden challenge				
	Up	Down	Left	Right	Center
CLR-C	4148.2	4331.6	4266.2	4229.2	4243.8
CLR-NC	3385.0	3453.2	3445.4	3401.2	3424.6
LR-C	4125.3	4297.5	4232.8	4203.5	4220.3
LR-NC	3362.1	3419.1	3411.9	3375.5	3401.1

above models we also created five instances for the five values of r_h for each model to get the average response time. When $r_h = 5$ (i.e., there is no pass-picture in the public challenge), we also created two further sub-models with and without the double scanning pattern, whose simulation results (response times) are then added up using the weights 0.66 and 0.34 to get the predicted average response time for the case of $r_h = 5$.

The results of the predicted average response time for all the four models are shown in Table 4.1, from which we can see the hidden challenge value corresponding to the smallest average response time is "Up" (consistently across all models), matching the findings reported in [21].

Based on the four models, we constructed a mixed probabilistic model where CLR-LR and N-NC patterns are considered based on different probabilities: 87% CLR and 13% LR for all challenge values; 40.9% C and 59.1% NC for "Up", 92.3% C and 7.7% NC for "Down", 64.7% C and 35.3% NC for "Left", 61.9% C and 38.1% NC for "Right", 46.2% C and 53.8% NC for "Center". The predicted average response time for each hidden challenge value of the mixed probabilistic model is shown in Fig. 4.6a, where the average response time for the hidden challenge value "Up" is significantly smaller than for other four values, which accords with the finding in [21].

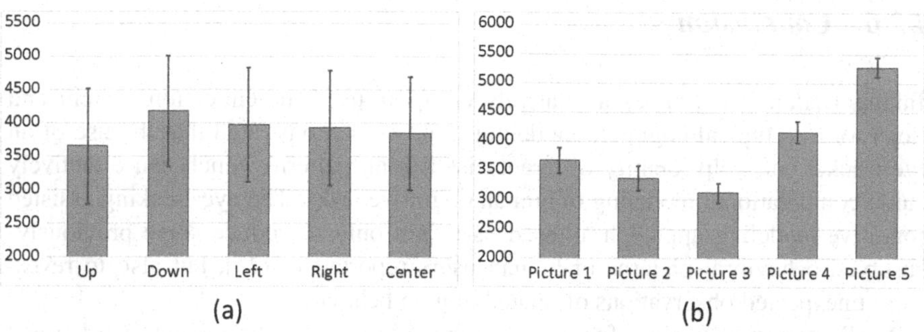

Fig. 4.6 Average response times (in milliseconds) for different values of (**a**) the hidden challenge c_h and (**b**) the hidden response r_h

We also looked at the average response times for different values of r_h and the results are shown in Fig. 4.6b. The results confirmed another observation in [21], which states that most users tended to respond more slowly when $r_h = 5$ (i.e., there is no pass-picture in the public challenge), and this could be explained by the double scanning pattern we described above. Furthermore, as identified in our eye-tracking experiment, in most cases participants adopted the CLR visual searching strategy for the pass-picture, and thus it is not surprising to observe that $r_h = 3$ (when the pass-picture is right in the middle of the public challenge panel) corresponds to the smallest average response time.

Comparing with the results reported in [21], there are still some noticeable differences. These differences could be caused by some subtle differences between our experimental setup and the one used in [21]. For instance, in the user study reported in [21], participants were allowed to use either mouse or keyboard to click the response button. However, for our models only mouse users are considered because keyboard users are more difficult to model due to various keyboard types and different individual human behaviors of using the keyboard. The smaller and different population of participants used in our experiment may be another source.

Our model could be further refined by considering the additional mental effort of converting r_h to r'_h. This will differ for different values of c_h because this conversion is effectively not needed for "Up" (the hidden challenge response button layout is "12345", which means $r'_h = r_h$). We thus can reasonably hypothesize that there will be less mental efforts for the "Up" case so that the response time is faster, which is also the main hypothesis Perković made in [21]. However, as demonstrated in the above results, the conversion process from r_h to r'_h is not the sole (may not be even the main) factor causing the observed non-uniform human behavior on average response time, which is a new insight obtained from our eye-tracking experiment. In our future work, we plan to investigate the conversion process from r_h to r'_h and see how that can be considered in the cognitive modeling task.

4.2.6 Conclusion

Taking Undercover [24] as a relatively complex user authentication system and CogTool as a typical cognitive modeling tool, we demonstrated that the use of an eye tracker can help identify different visual scan patterns which can effectively guide computational modeling of human cognitive tasks. The eye-tracking assisted cognitive modeling approach allowed us to not only reproduce some previously-observed behavioral patterns of human users reported in [21], but also to reveal more unexpected observations of related human behaviors.

While our work mainly focuses on a specific system, the insights we learned from the eye-tracking assisted cognitive modeling suggest eye-tracking should be used more widely in cognitive modeling of any cyber security systems with some visual elements in their UIs.

4.3 Case Studies: The Influence of Stimulus Type on Visual-Search Strategies Using Eye Tracking Data

In this section, we present our work on investigating how users perform a simple graphical authentication task with different types of graphical stimuli (faces, emojis, and elementary shapes) using an eye tracker. The main findings of this study include:

1. The image type as a variable has a significant effect on the user authentication time, showing that participants spent the longest time for faces, and were fastest with emojis.
2. The visual-search process is likely to start from the middle of an array of images regardless of the position of the target image.

These findings could shed light on our understanding of the impact of graphical stimuli on users' performance and visual-search strategies. We also believe these findings can be used by researchers and practitioners in different domains, including but not limited to image recognition-based user authentication.

4.3.1 Experimental Design

The main focus of this study is to assess the users' performance (reaction times) and scan paths/visual-search strategies via eye-tracking data for completing simple user authentication tasks with three different types of stimuli: *emojis*, *faces*, and elementary *shapes*.

4.3.1.1 Selection of Stimuli

Elementary shapes have been frequently used as stimuli in the experimental psychological work to study human visual-search system/behaviors [31, 35, 37]. However, elementary shapes are rarely used in graphical authentication systems. We believe that the reason is the limited number of elementary shapes that could be used in an authentication system to provide large enough password spaces. In this study, we included elementary shapes as stimuli as benchmark to compare with the other types of stimuli.

We selected faces in this study due to the following reasons:

- Faces have been used in the visual-search literature extensively, which has suggested that human beings are faster in encoding faces than non-face stimuli [15].
- According to previous work [26], familiar faces can be recognized even when the exposure duration is so short that other non-face objects cannot be identified.
- People can form an impression from a face presented only for as short as 100 ms [34].
- Faces are unique as their encoding is mandatory and their processing recruits specialized brain regions [32].
- previous research also identified that faces are more memorable for older users than younger users [20].
- Face-based graphical authentication systems has attracted lots of attention from both research and commercial communities.

Moreover, although some studies have used emojis in their systems [7, 11, 16], to the best of our knowledge, there is no previous psychological study that has systematically analyzed human users' visual-search strategies when emojis are used as targets.

4.3.1.2 Hypotheses

We conducted a lab-based experiment, in which each participant completed a task involving two stages: (1) the choice of a pass image per stimulus type (i.e., for each type of stimulus image, the user needs to choose one image as the password, we will refer to this as 'pass image' for the rest of this section); (2) the recognition of the pass image/no pass image (i.e., if the user cannot find the pass image, we will refer to this as 'no pass image' for the rest of this chapter) among an array of decoy images by pressing a button according to the pass image position. We tested the following main hypotheses:

- **H1**: the completion times and scan paths (i.e., we use 'scan paths' to refer to the eye gaze trajectory of visually searching the pass image) in the authentication task would vary as a function of the stimulus type (i.e., elementary shapes, faces, and emojis).

- **H2**: given the literature on the "central bias" [9, 10, 27, 28], participants would start their search for the pass image from the middle even when trials do not start with a central fixation marker [5].
- **H3**: the hypothesis is that the absence/presence of a pass image would significantly influence participants' completion times and scan paths in the authentication task based on the visual-search literature showing an asymmetry between the search for present vs. absent features [31, 35, 37]. In particular, we hypothesize that the presence of a pass image should be detected faster than its absence.

Both behavioral (reaction time) and eye-tracking (scan paths) data are analysed to test these hypotheses. This study aims to contribute to both the cyber security and the experimental psychology fields. We have no intention to propose yet another graphical authentication system and evaluate its usability and security. Instead, the focus of this study is to investigate the users' reaction times and oculomotor behaviors in an authentication-like setting to explore more general insights into the design of more secure and usable graphical authentication systems through an user-centric approach.

4.3.1.3 Participants

41 students (including undergraduate and postgraduate students), 31 female and 10 male, were recruited at the University of Surrey. They were aged from 21–32 ($M = 22$; $SD = 3.6$). Two rounds of recruitment took place across 4 months. 21 participants were recruited from the first round via poster advertisement, and 20 participants from the second round via an online system [25] used by the School of Psychology at the University of Surrey. Participants from the first round were rewarded with cash for their time based on the rate of 6 British pounds per hour. Participants from the second round (who were all students from the School of Psychology) were rewarded with lab tokens (i.e., credits for their undergraduate program). We did not collect any personal or sensitive data, and both rounds of the user study completed the University of Surrey Ethics Committee review process.[2]

4.3.1.4 Apparatus

Three types of stimuli (with 10 images per stimulus type) were used in this study: *emojis*, *faces*, and elementary *shapes*, shown in Fig. 4.7a–c, respectively. The *emojis* were obtained from the Unicode Emoji Charts [33]. The *faces* were acquired from

[2]University of Surrey Ethics Self-Assessment form with reference number: 160708-160702-20528369 (first round), and 160708-160702-26614408 (second round), which determines if the research meets the ethical review criteria of the University of Surrey's University Ethical Committee (UEC).

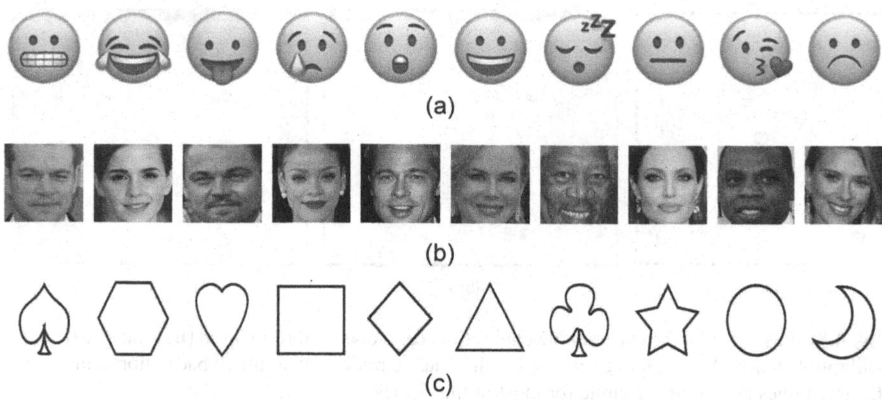

Fig. 4.7 Selected 10 images per stimulus type: (**a**) emojis, (**b**) faces, and (**c**) elementary shapes

the project 'cartoonfaces'[3] from the Centre for Visual Information Technology, International Institute of Information Technology, Hyderabad, India [18], and the *shapes* were downloaded from an online database used in [6].

The size of the stimuli was fixed at 75 pixels by 75 pixels in the registration phase, while it was 50 pixels by 50 pixels in the authentication phase, and the inter-stimuli distance was 50 pixels. The different stimulus size at the registration and authentication phases was deemed to reflect real-life fluctuations in the graphical features of electronic interfaces (e.g., due to screen rotation). In addition, the size difference remained identical across stimulus types, so it could not contribute to explain any differences in participant performance that we could observe across the face, emoji, and elementary shape conditions.

The machine used in the experiment was equipped with Intel(R) Core(TM) i5, 8GB RAM, and a 19 inch screen. A Tobii Pro X3-120 eye tracker was used for capturing eye gaze data. The sampling rate was 120 Hz, and the eye-tracking technique applied was corneal reflection, dark and bright pupil combination [30].

The eye tracker was mounted on the middle part of the screen bottom frame. We applied the following two recommendations to conduct all experiments: (a) the recommended distance from the participants' eyes to the eye tracker is between 60–65 cm for best eye-tracking performance; (b) the supporting distance recommended by the eye tracker manufacture is from 50 to 90 cm (more technical information about the eye tracker can be found at [30]).

[3]Available at: http://cvit.iiit.ac.in/images/Projects/cartoonFaces/IIIT-CFW1.0.zip

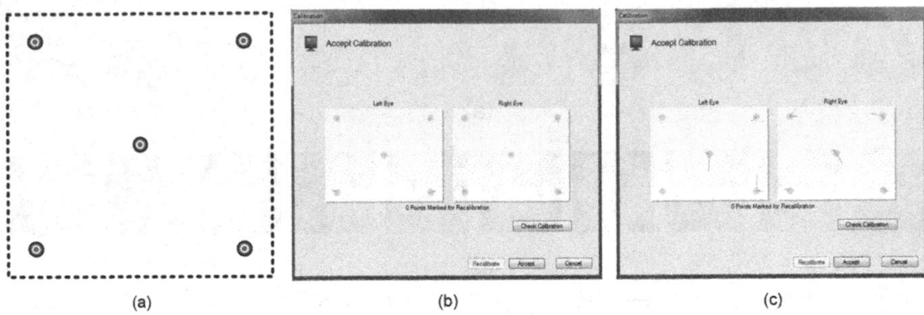

Fig. 4.8 Illustration of the eye tracking calibration. (a) 5 dots calibration grid (b) Example of good calibration, where the green lines are well within each circle (c) Example of bad calibration, where the green lines are out of the circle for most of the circles

4.3.1.5 Procedure

Participants from both rounds followed the same procedure encompassing briefing, training, calibration, registration and authentication. After reading the participant information sheet, a brief introduction was given to each participant at his/her arrival, then the participant was asked to sign the consent form, and fill in a simple demographics form. Next, each participant started the training session to practice and familiarize himself/herself with the software and the task for as long as he/she needed.

In the training phase, participants went through the whole process with the guidance of the experiment conductor. The authentication task required participants to respond to the stimulus displayed on the screen by pressing the corresponding key on the keyboard. As some participants did not remember where the key was, they tended to look at the keyboard to locate the key and then press.

We found out that participants could perform the authentication task without looking at the keyboard after practicing in the training phase for a while, which could eliminate/avoid this bias. For both training phase and experimental sessions, the same stimulus were used.

The calibration process took place after the training session, which required the participant to visually follow the moving red dot on the screen (see Fig. 4.8a), followed by a quality check of the eye tracking calibration results (see Fig. 4.8b, c). Then the participant could start the experiment.

We would like to address that in our study, we did not use a central fixation marker (for a similar procedure see [5]). This allowed us to investigate whether participants would spontaneously prefer certain spatial positions on the screen in keeping with the central fixation bias [9, 10, 27, 28] also in a user-authentication setting.

The task began with a registration phase. For each stimulus type, participants had to choose one as their pass image by clicking on them with the mouse. There were no time constraints, participants could spend as much time as they wanted to select their pass image as illustrated in Fig. 4.9a.

After the registration phase, each trial of the authentication phase consists of two steps. *Step 1*: the detection of the pass image among an image array containing 5 stimulus. The pass image could be either present or absent in the first four positions as illustrated in Fig. 4.9b; *Step 2*: after detecting if the pass image is present or absent, participants had to make correct response by pressing the correct button corresponding to the pass image position. The correct response is pressing button from 1 to 5 (i.e., if the pass image was detected at the first position of the image array, button '1' should be pressed on the keyboard; if the pass images was at the second position, button '2' should be pressed; and if the pass image was not present, button '5' should be pressed on the keyboard).

The experiment was designed to ensure each possible value of the correct response appeared 6 times randomly. There are 5 × 6 trials for each stimuli image type. In total, each participant completed 3 (stimuli image type) × 6 (repetition) × 5 (authentication trials) = 90 trials. In addition, the presentation order of the three blocks of the stimulus types was randomly set to avoid any order effect.

There was no time limit of how long the stimulus were displayed in each trial. Immediately after participants pressed the 'space' bar on the keyboard another trial started. Within this experiment setup, participants had the control of the speed of the experiment, and they could take a break between trials. However, according to our observations, no participants took any breaks between trials.

After finishing all the trials for one stimulus type, participants had the chance to take a break as long as they needed. Then participants repeated the same procedure for the two other stimulus types.

In the second round of the user study, we also conducted a followed-up semi-structured interview, aiming to get more insights into participants' strategies. The interviews did not follow a specific order, but they covered the following points:

- How are participants feeling after the study (distress, discomfort)?
- Were participants aware of using any specific method when searching for the pass image?
- Did participants use a different method for emojis, shapes, or faces?
- Did participants find a particular stimulus type more difficult than the others?

4.3.2 Results: User Performance

Two types of data were collected during the experiment:

- The user interaction data including mouse events, keyboard events, and timing information were collected in XML (eXtensible Markup Language) format, which will be referred to as "user performance data" for the rest of this section. The user performance data collected in XML format included the completion

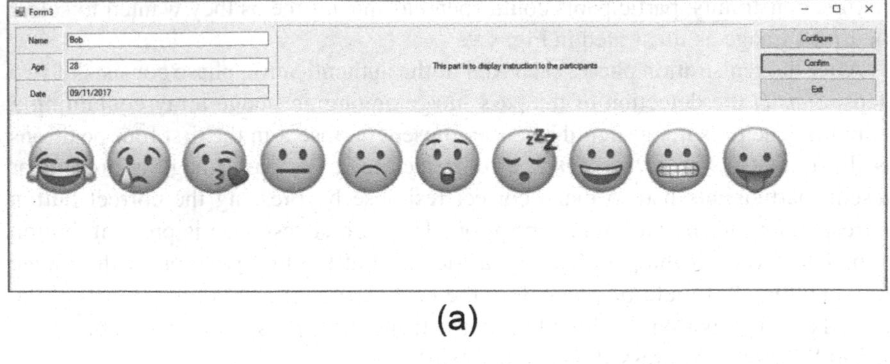

Position 1 Position 2 Position 3 Position 4 Position 5

(b)

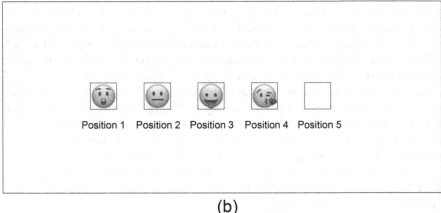

Fig. 4.9 Illustration of the software used in the experiment: (**a**) registration interface for participants to select pass image; (**b**) authentication screen for participants to identify the presence/absence of the selected pass image. The text in (**b**) is for illustration of the position only, it was not displayed in the experiment

time, the keyboard event which indicates the user response (pressed button), the correct position of pass image (ground truth), and the stimulus type.

- Eye-tracking data including time-stamp, on screen coordinates, and screen video recording data were collected via the Tobii Studio software [29]. We implemented several MATLAB scripts to work with Tobii Studio [29] for eye-tracking data handling, refinement, and analysis.

We tested the possible effects of the stimulus types on users' reaction times and visual-search strategies. The findings from the two rounds of the study were consistent with each other. As the settings and experimental procedures were the same for the two rounds of data collection, we will present the analysis of the merged data.

Table 4.2 Descriptive statistics for pass image position

Pass image position	Mean (ms)	Standard deviation
Position 1	991.04	338.84
Position 2	1010.45	365.82
Position 3	1150.80	448.63
Position 4	1254.23	505.24
No pass image	1343.36	467.79

Table 4.3 Descriptive statistics for stimuli image type

Stimuli image type	Mean (ms)	Standard deviation
Emoji	1064.96	440.30
Face	1145.61	449.41
Shape	1094.32	437.64

4.3.2.1 Effects of Stimulus Type and Pass Image Position

The user performance data of the first participant was missing due to a software issue and thus we present our analyses for the data of 40 participants. In this part of the analysis, we were more interested in gaining insights into the possible impact of stimulus types and the pass image position on user performance. The trials containing no pass image would be irrelevant, and thus we excluded these data, resulting in a data set of 2,880 reads = 40 (participants) × 3 (stimuli image type) × 6 (repetition) × 4 (pass image position).

The basic descriptive statistics are shown in Tables 4.2 and 4.3. Participants were faster when they had to recognize emojis than faces and elementary shapes. With regards to the position of the pass image, participants reacted the fastest when the pass image appeared at position 1, and slowest at position 4.

We carried out a 3 (stimulus types: faces vs. emojis, vs. elementary shapes) × 4 (position: first vs. second vs. third vs. fourth) repeated-measures Analysis of Variance (ANOVA) with the completion time as the dependent variable. The completion time was measured from stimulus appearance on the screen to when a key pressed event was detected. The main effect of stimulus types ($F(2, 39) = 8.674$, $p = 0.0002$) was significant.

However, the effect size was small (partial $\eta^2 = 0.006$), which could be due to the relatively small sample size. Nevertheless, we conducted post-hoc Tukey-Kramer tests (see Tables 4.4 and 4.5). Results indicated that there was a significant difference in completion time between *emojis* and *faces*, while there was no significant difference between *emoji* and *elementary shapes*, and between *faces* and *elementary shapes*. Participants spent approximately 100 ms more on average to complete each trial for *faces* than *emojis* (see Fig. 4.10a).

The main effect of the pass image position ($F(3, 39) = 60.195$, $p = 0.000$) was also significant. Its effect size was small to medium (partial $\eta^2 = 0.059$), thus larger than the effect size of stimulus type, suggesting that stimuli position had a stronger effect on users' completion time than stimulus type.

Table 4.4 Tukey-Kramer pairwise comparison between stimulus types

Pairwise comparison	p-value
Emoji vs. Face	0.000
Emoji vs Shape	0.292
Face vs. Shape	0.024

Table 4.5 Tukey-Kramer pairwise comparison between pass image positions

Pairwise comparison	p-value	Pairwise comparison	p-value
Position 1 vs. position 2	0.826	Position 2 vs. position 3	0.000
Position 1 vs. position 3	0.000	Position 2 vs. position 4	0.000
Position 1 vs. position 4	0.000	Position 3 vs. position 4	0.000

Moreover, we conducted the pairwise comparisons (see Table 4.5) that indicated significant differences between all pass image positions except for the 'position 1 vs. position 2' comparison. As shown in Fig. 4.10b, participants spent the shortest time to identify the pass image if the pass image appeared at position 1, and there was little difference between position 1 and position 2. Participants spent the longest time to find the pass image when it appeared at position 4. The stimulus type by position interaction ($F(6, 39) = 1.035$, $p = 0.4$) was not significant.

4.3.2.2 Effect of Presence/Absence Condition

This section compares the user performance data between trials that contained a pass image (these will be referred to as the presence condition) and trials that did not have any pass image (these will be referred to as the absence condition). As illustrated in Fig. 4.9c, 'position 1', 'position 2', 'position 3', and 'position 4' are positions that belong to the presence condition, and 'position 5' is the position corresponding to the absence condition.

We designed the experiment so that pass images appeared at each position randomly the same number of times. Therefore, the number of trials in the presence condition was 4 times as the number of trials in the absence condition. We subdivided the data of the presence condition into 4 subsets, whereby each subset had the equal size of the data of the absence condition. We used a dummy variable condition (C) to indicate the presence and absence conditions. Dummy variable value of '1' means presence condition, and '0' represents absence condition.

Then we performed a 3 (stimulus types: faces vs. emojis, vs. elementary shapes) × 2 (condition: presence vs. absence) repeated-measures ANOVA on completion times for each of the four cases. Each case included one subset of data for the presence condition, and another (of equal size) for the absence condition. The statistical results are depicted in Table 4.6.

There was a significant main effect of the condition for all cases (see Table 4.7). Referring to Table 4.3, participants spent approximately 200–300 ms more on

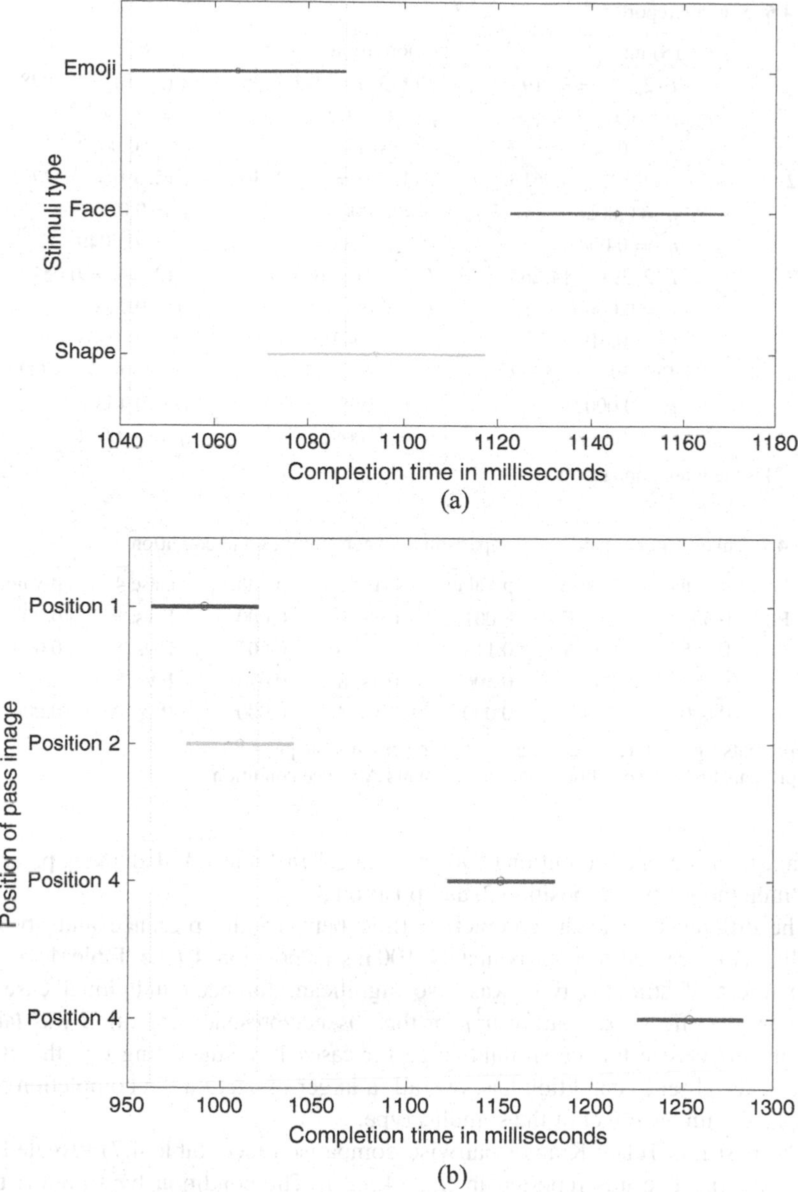

Fig. 4.10 Comparison of completion times for different factor, where the blue group is the base group for comparison, and red group has significant difference comparing with the base group. (**a**) Different stimuli. (**b**) Different positions of pass image

Table 4.6 Statistic report

	(S)timuli	(C)ondition	S × C
Case 1	$F(2, 39) = 8.1199$ $p = 0.0003$ $\eta^2 = 0.011$	$F(1, 39) = 243.7635$ $p = 0.0000$ $\eta^2 = 0.1453$	$F(2, 39) = 2.2978$ $p = 0.1009$ $\eta^2 = 0.0032$
Case 2	$F(2, 39) = 5.9616$ $p = 0.0026$ $\eta^2 = 0.0082$	$F(1, 39) = 227.3346$ $p = 0.0000$ $\eta^2 = 0.1382$	$F(2, 39) = 3.5273$ $p = 0.0296$ $\eta^2 = 0.0049$
Case 3	$F(2, 39) = 14.263$ $p = 0.0000$ $\eta^2 = 0.0195$	$F(1, 39) = 63.688$ $p = 0.0000$ $\eta^2 = 0.0425$	$F(2, 39) = 0.0579$ $p = 0.9437$ $\eta^2 = 0.0008$
Case 4	$F(2, 39) = 8.5377$ $p = 0.0002$ $\eta^2 = 0.0118$	$F(1, 39) = 11.867$ $p = 0.0006$ $\eta^2 = 0.0082$	$F(2, 39) = 0.7909$ $p = 0.4536$ $\eta^2 = 0.0011$

[S × C] is the interaction effect

Table 4.7 Tukey-Kramer pairwise comparison between stimulus and condition

Case 1	p-value	Case 2	p-value	Case 3	p-value	Case 4	p-value
E vs. F	0.000	E vs.F	0.001	E vs. F	0.000	E vs. F	0.000
E vs. S	0.155	E vs.S	0.118	E vs. S	0.005	E vs. S	0.079
F vs. S	0.074	F vs.S	0.306	F vs. S	0.076	F vs. S	0.118
P vs. A	0.000	P vs.A	0.000	P vs. A	0.000	P vs. A	0.000

E represents Emoji, F represents Face, and S represents Shape
P represents Presence condition, and A represents Absence condition

average in the absence condition ("No pass image" in Table 4.3) than in the presence condition (at position 1, position 2, and position 3).

The difference in mean completion time between the presence and absence conditions decreased to approximately 100 ms at position 4 (see Table 4.3). The main effect of stimulus type was also significant for each individual case. In addition, the effect size (partial η^2) for the absence/presence condition was larger than the effect size for the stimulus type for cases 1–3, suggesting that the effect of presence/absence condition has, overall, a larger impact on the completion time compared with the effect of the stimulus type.

The post-hoc Tukey-Kramer pairwise comparison (see Table 4.7) revealed the same pattern of results reported in Sect. 4.3.2.1. The condition by stimulus type interaction effect was not significant except for case 2.

4.3.3 *Results: Visual Search*

In addition to the analysis of the user performance data, this part focuses on analyzing the eye gaze data extracted from the eye tracker, particularly the fixation data to investigate the users' visual-search strategies.

4.3.3.1 Fixations Heat Map

Fixation is the central fovea vision on a single location for a period of time so that the visual system can take in detailed information about what is being looked at. The fixation duration threshold used in this experiment is 70 ms. As depicted in Fig. 4.11, the fixation heat maps present the visual representation of the distribution of the fixation data extracted from the eye gaze data in relation to the stimuli and pass image position.

Each heat map aggregates the absolute fixation duration for all participants, and it depicts the amount of fixations for each stimulus type. The warmer the color is, the longer the time spent on the area (e.g., areas highlighted in red have longer fixation time than areas highlighted in green). The fixations heat maps revealed that participants had the longest absolute fixation duration on the position (Positions 1 to 4) at which the pass image was present regardless of the stimulus type.

This suggests that participants spent more time on pass images to make inferences about cognitive processes or suggesting interests of probing, which could be the process of identifying and recognizing the stimuli. In contrast, the pattern in the absence condition (i.e., no pass image) was more diversified, which reveals that participants spent a fair amount of time on checking each presented stimulus in a serial fashion.

4.3.3.2 First Fixation

First fixation is the first time participants look at a stimuli more than a specified fixation duration threshold (70 ms) for each trial. We were interested in investigating the relationship between the fist fixation and the pass image position, which could give us some insights of how participants started the visual-search process.

Relationship Between the Pass Image Position and First Fixation for the Same Trial

Figure 4.12 illustrates the first fixation probability heat map. The number in each cell is the probability that the first fixation would land on a position given a pass image position. The first row of the figure shows that if the pass image is at position 1, there is 34% and 30% chance that a participant's first fixation would land at

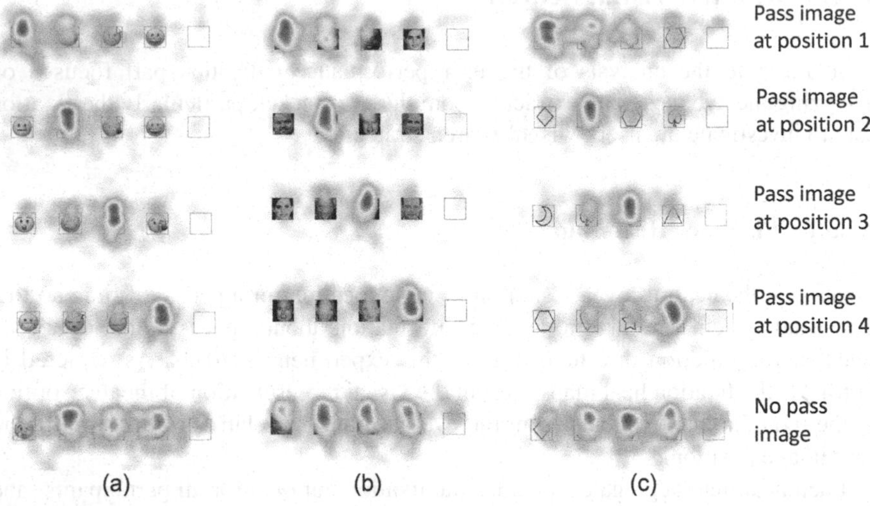

Fig. 4.11 Fixations heat map for different stimuli

position 2 and position 3, respectively, while less than 20% probability that the first fixation would be at either position 1 or position 4, and only 2% probability that a participant would start her/his visual-search process from position 5. As participants were aware that there was no stimuli presented at position 5, the lowest probability of their first fixation being at position 5 is not surprising. This pattern of results is consistent across the other pass image positions. In general, there was a higher chance that participants started their visual-search process from position 2 or position 3 compared to position 1 and position 4 regardless of the pass image position. Moreover, we also looked at the first fixation probability heat map for each stimulus type individually, and we found similar results.

Correlation Between Pass Image Position in the Previous Trial and First Fixation at the Current Trial

During the experiment, we observed that all participants completed all trials without any break (even though they were allowed to). Thus, we looked at the data to extract the time difference in-between trials. The mean break time and its standard deviation are 160.63 ms and 104.25 for face images; 227.30 ms and 202.81 for emoji images; 156.67 ms and 57.33 for shape images.

Hence, we hypothesized that the starting position of the visual-search process of the present trial could be influenced by the pass image position from the previous trial. Then, we produced a heat map as shown in Fig. 4.13 to visualize this relationship.

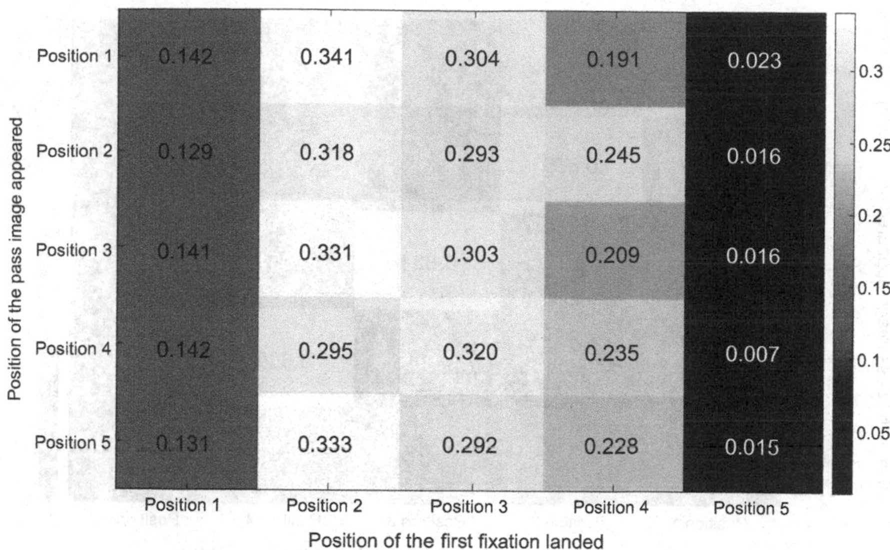

Fig. 4.12 First fixation probability heat map for all stimuli image types, the lighter the color is, the higher the probability is and vice versa

The y-axis denotes the pass image position from the previous trial, and the x-axis indicates the position of the first fixation at the present trial. The number in each cell is the probability that the participant's first fixation would land at that position given a pass image position from the previous trial. The first row of the figure shows that given that the pass image appeared at position 1 in the previous trial, the probabilities that the first fixation lands at position 1 and position 2 in the current trial are approximately 61% and 30%, respectively. If the pass image appeared at position 2 in the previous trial, the probability of having first fixations at position 2 and position 3 in the current trial were 88% and 10%, respectively.

Moreover, by looking at the whole heat map, there is a clear light color diagonal line across the heat map, suggesting that there could be a close correlation between the pass image position from the previous trial and the position of the first fixation at the present trial. We calculated the correlation coefficient ($r = 0.809$) without the "no pass" image (last row and last column), which indicates that there is a strong correlation between the position of the pass image from previous trial and the starting position of visual search in the present trial. Nevertheless, the probabilities are still higher for the middle positions, which is in line with our previous finding indicating the presence of a central fixation bias.

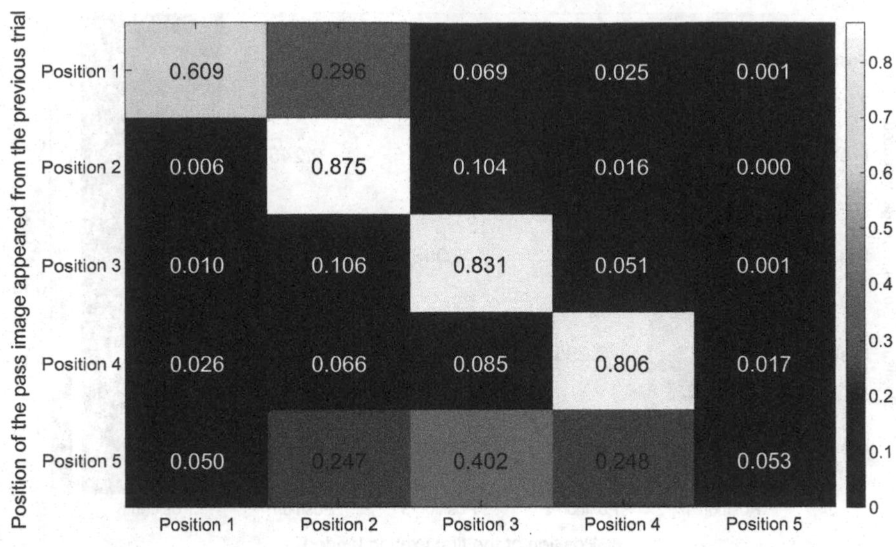

Fig. 4.13 Correlation between pass image position from the previous trial and first fixation position at current trial. The lighter the color is, the higher the probability is and vice versa

4.3.3.3 Visual Search After First Fixation

First fixation is the first time participants look at a stimuli more than a specified fixation duration threshold (70 ms) for each trial. Here, we are interested in analyzing participants' fixations after the first fixation. We classified the subsequent fixations into three groups: (1) shift fixation to the image on the left-hand side of the first fixation image; (2) stay at the first fixed image; and (3) shift fixation to the image on the right-hand side of the first fixation image. We reshaped the data and summarized participants' visual-search strategies after the first fixation in relation to the pass image position in Table 4.8.

Given that the pass image is at position 1 (i.e., the row of 'Pass image at pos.1'), if the participant had the first fixation at position 1, the probability of shifting the fixation to the image on the right-hand side (i.e., position 2) was 0.38, while the probability of remaining fixated at position 1 was 0.62; if the participant had the first fixation at position 2, the probability of subsequently shifting the fixation to the left, right, and stay at the same position was 0.67, 0.21, and 0.12, respectively; if the first fixation was at positions 3 and 4, the probabilities of moving the fixation to the left increased to 0.91 and 0.95, respectively. From the observation of data for other pass image positions (i.e., row 2, 3, 4 from Table 4.8), participants were likely to shift their fixations directly towards the pass image position regardless of the first fixation position.

Table 4.8 Transition probability after the first fixation

	1st fixation at pos.1			1st fixation at pos.2			1st fixation at pos.3			1st fixation at pos.4			1st fixation at pos.5		
	L	R	S	L	R	S	L	R	S	L	R	S	L	R	S
Pass image at pos.1	0.00	0.38	0.62	0.67	0.21	0.12	0.91	0.03	0.07	0.95	0.00	0.05	0.00	0.00	1.00
Pass image at pos.2	0.00	0.99	0.01	0.10	0.14	0.75	0.93	0.03	0.04	0.99	0.00	0.01	0.00	0.00	1.00
Pass image at pos.3	0.00	0.98	0.02	0.07	0.86	0.07	0.97	0.03	0.67	0.97	0.00	0.03	0.09	0.00	0.91
Pass image at pos.4	0.00	0.99	0.01	0.09	0.88	0.03	0.50	0.61	0.08	0.50	0.00	0.50	0.00	0.00	1.00
No pass image	0.00	0.98	0.02	0.27	0.68	0.05	0.95	0.11	0.09	0.95	0.00	0.05	0.00	0.00	1.00

[L] indicates the next fixation shifts to the image on the left hand side of first fixation image
[R] indicates the next fixation shifts to the image on the right hand side of first fixation image
[S] indicates the next fixation remains at the same position

4.3.3.4 Scan Paths

This part focuses on the analysis of the participants' fixation sequence, that is, their scan paths. We clustered the data as a function of the participants' fixation sequences and listed the top 5 most frequently used fixation sequences depicted in Tables 4.9 to 4.12 for each pass image position, respectively.

The start of the red arrows shown in the tables represents the first fixation position, and the tip of the arrows represents the final fixation position. For instance, if we look at the top 5 fixation sequences for pass image position 1 (see Table 4.9), '21' means that participants started visual-search process at position 2, and then finished their visual-search task at position 1. 20% of participants used '21', while 12% of them used '321' for the visual-search task, and interestingly 8% of participants directly identified the pass image at position 1 without looking at stimulus presented at other positions. By looking at other pass image positions, it is interesting to notice that more than 10% of participants could directly identify the pass image (23% for pass image position 2, 20% for pass image position 3, and 12% for pass image position 4). By looking at the top 5 fixation sequences for all pass image positions, participants can directly shift their attention to the pass image using the shortest paths regardless of the first fixation position for most cases (exceptions are fixation sequence '423' for pass image at position 3, fixation sequence '324' for pass image at position 4).

Table 4.9 Top 5 fixation sequences (visual-search strategy) for pass image at position 1

Top 5	Fixation sequences	Mean time (ms)	Percentage
1st	'21' : 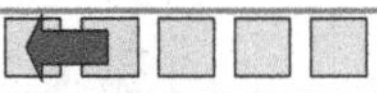	877	20%
2nd	'321' : 	1064	12%
3rd	'1' : 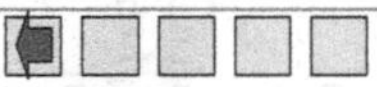	819	8%
4th	'31' : 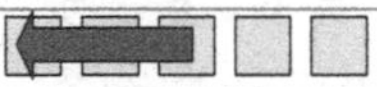	929	8%
5th	'421' : 	1093	7%
Overall percentage			55%

Table 4.10 Top 5 fixation sequences (visual-search strategy) for pass image at position 2

Top 5	Fixation sequences	Mean time (ms)	Percentage
1st	'2' : 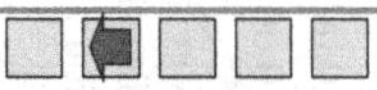	809	23%
2nd	'32' : 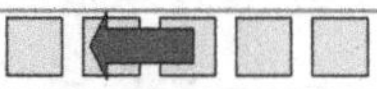	959	23%
3rd	'42' : 	1104	13%
4th	'12' : 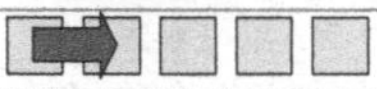	964	9%
5th	'432' : 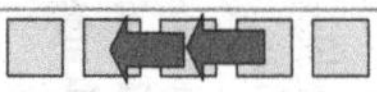	1211	6%
Overall percentage			74%

Table 4.11 Top 5 fixation sequences (visual-search strategy) for pass image at position 3

Top 5	Fixation sequences	Mean time (ms)	Percentage
1st	'23' :	1059	23%
2nd	'3' :	885	20%
3rd	'43' :	1253	10%
4th	'13' :	1176	6%
5th	'423' :	1310	6%
Overall percentage			65%

Table 4.12 Top 5 fixation sequences (visual-search strategy) for pass image at position 4

Top 5	Fixation sequences	Mean time (ms)	Percentage
1st	'34' :	1127	17%
2nd	'4' :	918	12%
3rd	'24' :	1254	11%
4th	'234' :	1372	9%
5th	'324' :	1299	6%
Overall percentage			55%

This finding indicates that the presence of the pass image "popped out". The longer the fixation sequence, the more mean completion time is needed. Thus, this results is line with the faster completion time in the presence compared to the absence condition. It is also consistent with the observation revealed from the transition probability (see Table 4.8).

Moreover, the overall percentage of top 5 scan paths for each pass image position indicates that 55% of participants used the 5 most frequently used scan paths to find the pass image for pass image position 1, and the percentages are 74%, 65%, and 55% for pass image positions 2, 3, and 4, respectively. These high percentages justify our selection of the top 5 most frequently used fixation sequences as representation of scan paths.

Furthermore, the length of the fixation sequence could be used as an indicator of the effort required to complete the visual-search task. We investigated the average fixation sequence length needed to identify the pass image at each position. A similar length of fixation sequences for pass image at positions 1 and 4 was needed, for which participants fixated 2.5 times before confirming the pass image position. The length of fixation sequences is relative shorter for pass image at positions 2 and 3, for which participants fixated approximately 2 times before identifying the pass image. This is in line with the observation that participants were more likely to start their visual-search process from these two positions. In the case of the absence of the pass image, participants made over three fixations on average before confirming that there was no pass image.

4.3.4 Discussion

The present study aimed at investigating the effects of different types of stimuli (e.g., faces images vs. emojis vs. elementary shapes) on human visual-search strategies within a user authentication setting. In this section, we will discuss both the user performance data and participants' scan paths extracted from eye-tracking data in relation to the hypotheses laid out in Sect. 4.3.1.2.

The Role of Different Stimulus Types

The social cognitive literature has long shown the relevance of faces for human beings [2, 17]. The results showed that the stimulus type had significant effect on participants' completion time. As previous research has shown that the neural processing of familiar faces takes places as fast as 140 ms [3] and some people are able to detect certain faces presented for 33 ms [22], we hypothesized that people would react fastest to the *Face* stimulus.

It was surprising to find out that people spent more time on trials with faces as opposed to the other two stimulus types (participants identified *Emoji* stimulus the fastest). However research [20] discovered that only older participants improved performance with face-based authentication system compared to non-face systems. As the sample for this experiment made up of younger participants, this could be the cause that faces images did not facilitate their performance.

The follow-up interviews in the second round data collection gave us more insights into this unexpected finding. For question 'Did participants find a particular stimulus more difficult than the others?', 11 out of 20 participants felt that *faces* were the most difficult stimuli image type, and 7 out of 20 participants felt that *elementary shapes* were the most difficult type. On the other hand, only 1 out of 20 participants had difficulty with *emojis*. This is in line with statistical results on completion times.

In addition, the responses to three other questions listed in Sect. 4.3.1.5 revealed that participants used specific strategies to select and identify *emoji* pass images. Participants preferred to select an *emoji* pass image that had a distinctive color feature such as the red heart or blue tears shown in Fig. 4.7a. These features could grab the participants' attention by means of a pop-out effect. In contrast, *faces* had more complex features compared with *emojis* and *elementary shapes*, so that participants could have find it more difficult to recognize them than emojis.

In contrast with *emojis* and *faces*, *elementary shapes* were monochrome images. They did not have the distinctive color features, but they had simpler features than *faces*. This might explain why the mean completion time for *elementary shape* was in-between *emojis* and *faces*.

Presence-Absence Asymmetry in Visual Search

The psychological literature has also long shown a presence-absence asymmetry in human beings' visual search, whereby present stimuli are processed faster and in parallel (they thus "pop out"), while absent stimuli are processed slower and serially, that is, they require an item by item check for the absence of a relevant feature [31, 35]. In line with this literature, we put forward **H3**. The results supported our hypothesis. Indeed, the effect of absence/presences of the pass image on the completion time was found to be significant.

Participants spent significant more time when the pass image was absent than when the pass image was present. The fixation heat map presented in Fig. 4.11 indicates that the fixation patterns are more diversified in the absence condition. In particular, it suggests that participants tended to individually check all presented stimulus before deciding that the pass image was indeed absent. This is in line with the serial processing already identified for the absence of features in the psychological work such as in [31].

Within a user authentication setting, this finding might also be explained by the double scan behavior described in our recent work [36], which suggests that users are likely to scan all stimuli repeatedly when the target stimulus is absent. An important caveat about this finding is that the presence-absence asymmetry we found could parallel the significant main effect of pass image position indicating increasing completion times for pass images in the left to right direction (see Sect. 4.3.2.1). Since the "no pass" image was always the right most, there is a need of future research to disentangle the possible overlapping effects of position and absence.

Central Bias

We explored the data on first fixations to investigate how participants started their visual search. We hypothesized (**H2**) that participants would start their search from the middle positions of the array, even if there was not a central fixation marker at the start of each trial, in line with [5].

The results presented in Fig. 4.11 suggest that participants' first fixations tended to land on stimulus at middle positions (i.e., position 2 and position 3) of the array, which is in keeping with the literature on the "central fixation bias" [5, 9, 10, 27, 28]. This is also partially in line with the findings in our recent work [36], which showed that more than half of human participants in a user authentication experiment started their visual search from the center position of an array of images.

In addition, the findings of a strong correlation between the pass image position from a previous trial and the first fixation point in the current trial (see Fig. 4.13) could reveal potential weaknesses and vulnerable aspects in similar graphical user authentication systems.

These insights could be explored to build adversary models to a graphical user authentication system that requires users to repeatedly and quickly identify pass images from an array of images. On the other hand, these could be also used to propose feasible countermeasure to mitigate such attacks.

The qualitative data from the interviews revealed that the subjective views of how participants visually searched their pass image were diverse, including '*Search start from the middle*', '*look at the beginning from left to right*', and '*look at all at one go*' etc. However, there were no dominant strategies self-reported by the participants.

Moreover, scan paths data (see Tables 4.9, 4.10, 4.11, and 4.12) suggest that the majority of participants could directly shift their fixation towards the pass image using the shortest possible scan paths regardless of the first fixation position and pass image position. This occurred when the pass image was present (in one of the first four positions). Thus, this finding is line with the pop-out effect of the presence of stimuli that are processed in parallel [31]. This finding can also be explained by considering the human peripheral vision, which allows participants to be aware of the images adjacent to the fixated one. If images are placed further apart, fewer images can appear within the peripheral vision, and that could influence people's scan paths. Future research could deepen the investigation of the impact of inter-stimuli distance on visual search.

4.3.5 Conclusion

This study applied principles from the psychological literature on visual search to investigate people's visual-search strategies in the context of a simple graphical authentication task using *emojis*, *faces*, and *elementary shapes*.

The results showed that participants were fastest in completing the task when *emojis* were used, and they were slowest when *faces* were presented. This is a surprising finding in light of the social cognitive literature that indicates people's sensitivity to faces, which could be quickly detected [22]. Consistently, the qualitative data from the interviews with participants indicated that *emojis* had more distinctive features that could produce effect similar to pop-up effects that allow participants to recognize stimuli quicker and through parallel processing [31].

In addition, our results corroborate those on the 'central bias' [5]. Indeed, participants were more likely to start their visual search with first fixations on stimulus placed at middle positions of the array of images regardless of the position of their pass image. Furthermore, in line with the presence-absence asymmetry in visual search described in the psychological literature [31, 35], when the pass image was absent participants scanned all stimulus serially and repeatedly to make sure that there was no pass image, and hence spent more time to complete the task. Conversely, the presence of a pass image induced a fast, parallel visual search.

Finally, the findings of a strong correlation between the pass image position in the previous trial and the first fixation position in the current trial provided insights into potential attacks based on pass images' positions as well as information that can be used to design more secure and usable graphical user authentication systems.

References

1. Alsharnouby, M., Alaca, F., Chiasson, S.: Why phishing still works: user strategies for combating phishing attacks. Int. J. Hum.-Comput. Stud. **82**, 69–82 (2015)
2. Bahrick, H., Bahrick, P., Wittlinger, R.: Fifty years of memory for names and faces: a cross-sectional approach. J. Exp. Psychol. Gen. **104**(1), 54–75 (1975)
3. Barragan-Jason, G., Cauchoix, M., Barbeau, E.: The neural speed of familiar face recognition. Neuropsychologia **75**(Supplement C), 390–401 (2015)
4. Byrne, M.D., Anderson, J.R., Douglass, S., Matessa, M.: Eye tracking the visual search of click-down menus. In: Proceedings of 1999 SIGCHI Conference on Human Factors in Computing Systems (CHI'99), pp. 402–409. ACM (1999)
5. Canosa, R., Pelz, J., Mennie, N., Peak, J.: High-level aspects of oculomotor control during viewing of natural-task images. In: Human Vision and Electronic Imaging VIII. Proceedings of SPIE – the International Society for Optical Engineering, vol. 5007, pp. 240–251 (2003)
6. Chanceaux, M., Mathôt, S., Grainger, J.: Normative-ratings experiment for flanker stimuli, figshare. Online dataset (2014). https://doi.org/10.6084/m9.figshare.977864.v1
7. Cocozza, P.: Crying with laughter: how we learned how to speak emoji. Online document (2015). http://www.richardhartley.com/2015/11/crying-with-laughter-how-we-learned-how-to-speak-emoji/
8. Fleetwood, M.D., Byrne, M.D.: Modeling the visual search of displays: a revised ACT-R model of icon search based on eye-tracking data. Hum.-Comput. Interact. **21**(2), 153–197
9. Foulsham, T., Underwood, G.: What can saliency models predict about eye movements? spatial and sequential aspects of fixations during encoding and recognition. J. Vis. **8**(2), 6 (2008)
10. Foulsham, T., Walker, E., Kingstone, A.: The where, what and when of gaze allocation in the lab and the natural environment. Vis. Res. **51**(17), 1920–1931 (2011)
11. Golla, M., Detering, D., Durmuth, M.: EmojiAuth: quantifying the security of emoji-based authentication. In: Proceedings of 2017 Workshop on Usable Security (USEC) (2017). https://www.ndss-symposium.org/ndss2017/usec-mini-conference-programme/emojiauth-quantifying-security-emoji-based-authentication/
12. Hornof, A.J.: Cognitive strategies for the visual search of hierarchical computer displays. Hum.-Comput. Interact. **10**(3), 183–223 (2004)
13. Hornof, A.J., Halverson, T.: Cognitive strategies and eye movements for searching hierarchical computer displays. In: Proceedings of 2003 SIGCHI Conference on Human Factors in Computing Systems (CHI 2003), pp. 249–256. ACM (2003)
14. John, B., Prevas, K., Salvucci, D., Koedinger, K.: Predictive human performance modeling made easy. In: Proceedings of the SIGCHI Conference on Human Factors in Computing Systems, CHI'04, pp. 455–462. ACM, New York (2004). http://doi.acm.org/10.1145/985692.985750
15. Liu, J., Harris, A., Kanwisher, N.: Stages of processing in face perception: an meg study. Nat. Neurosci. **5**(9), 910–6 (2002)
16. Locke, C.: Emoji passcodes – seriously fun, seriously secure. Online document (2015). https://www.iedigital.com/fintech-news-insight/fintech-security-regulation/emoji-passcodes-seriously-fun-seriously-secure/
17. Mckone, E., Kanwisher, N., Duchaine, B.C.: Can generic expertise explain special processing for faces? Trends Cogn. Sci. **11**(1), 8–15 (2007)

18. Mishra, A., Rai, N., Mishra, A., Jawahar, C.: IIIT-CFW: a benchmark database of cartoon faces in the wild (2016). https://cvit.iiit.ac.in/research/projects/cvit-projects/cartoonfaces
19. Miyamoto, D., Blanc, G., Kadobayashi, Y.: Eye can tell: on the correlation between eye movement and phishing identification. In: Neural Information Processing: 22nd International Conference, ICONIP 2015, Istanbul, 9–12 Nov 2015, Proceedings Part III. Lecture Notes in Computer Science, vol. 9194, pp. 223–232. Springer (2015)
20. Nicholson, J., Coventry, L., Briggs, P.: Faces and pictures: understanding age differences in two types of graphical authentications. Int. J. Hum.-Comput. Stud. **71**(10), 958–966 (2013)
21. Perković, T., Li, S., Mumtaz, A., Khayam, S., Javed, Y., Čagalj, M.: Breaking undercover: exploiting design flaws and nonuniform human behavior. In: Proceedings of the Seventh Symposium on Usable Privacy and Security, SOUPS'11, pp. 5:1–5:15. ACM, New York (2011). http://doi.acm.org/10.1145/2078827.2078834
22. Pessoa, L., Japee, S., Ungerleider, L.G.: Visual awareness and the detection of fearful faces. Emotion **5**(2), 243–247 (2005)
23. Rao, R.P.N., Zelinsky, G.J., Hayhoe, M.M., Ballard, D.H.: Eye movements in iconic visual search. Vis. Res. **42**(11), 1447–1463 (2002)
24. Sasamoto, H., Christin, N., Hayashi, E.: Undercover: authentication usable in front of prying eyes. In: Proceedings of 2008 SIGCHI Conference on Human Factors in Computing Systems (CHI 2008), pp. 183–192. ACM (2008)
25. Sona System Ltd: Psychology Research Participation System. Website. https://surrey-uk.sona-systems.com/
26. Tanaka, J.: The entry point of face recognition: evidence for face expertise. J. Exp. Psychol. **130**(3), 534–543 (2001)
27. Tatler, B.: The central fixation bias in scene viewing: selecting an optimal viewing position independently of motor biases and image feature distributions. J. Vis. **7**(14), 4 (2007)
28. Tatler, B., Baddeley, R., Gilchrist, I.: Visual correlates of fixation selection: effects of scale and time. Vis. Res. **45**(5), 643–659 (2005)
29. Tobii AB: Tobii Studio User's Manual. Online document, Version 3.4.5 (2016). https://www.tobiipro.com/siteassets/tobii-pro/user-manuals/tobii-pro-studio-user-manual.pdf
30. Tobii AB: Tobii Pro X3-120 eye tracker user manual. Online document, Version 1.0.7 (2017). https://www.tobiipro.com/siteassets/tobii-pro/user-manuals/tobii-pro-x3-120-user-manual.pdf/?v=1.0.7
31. Treisman, A., Souther, J.: Search asymmetry: a diagnostic for preattentive processing of separable features. J. Exp. Psychol. **114**(3), 285–310 (1985)
32. Tsao, D., Livingstone, M.: Mechanisms of face perception. Ann. Rev. Neurosci. **31**, 411–437 (2008)
33. Unicode: Unicode ® Emoji Charts v5.0. Online document. http://unicode.org/emoji/charts/full-emoji-list.html
34. Willis, J., Todorov, A.: First impressions. Psychol. Sci. **17**(7), 592–598 (2006)
35. Wolfe, J.: Asymmetries in visual search: an introduction. Percept. Psychophys. **63**(3), 381–389 (2001)
36. Yuan, H., Li, S., Rusconi, P., Aljaffan, N.: When eye-tracking meets cognitive modeling: applications to cyber security systems. In: Human Aspects of Information Security, Privacy and Trust: 5th International Conference, HAS 2017, Held as Part of HCI International 2017, Vancouver, 9–14 July 2017, Proceedings. Lecture Notes in Computer Science, vol. 10292, pp. 251–264. Springer, Cham (2017)
37. Zelinsky, G., Sheinberg, D.: Eye movements during parallel–serial visual search. J. Exp. Psychol. Hum. Percept. Perform. **23**(1), 244–262 (1997)

Chapter 5
Large-Scale Human Performance Modeling Framework

Abstract This chapter presents a proposed conceptual framework to address the issues and challenges of large-scale cognitive modeling. UI/UX designers are considered as the main target users of the framework with additional support from computer programmers and psychologists. The framework has the following features: (1) it supports high-level parameterization; (2) it supports automation; (3) it supports modeling dynamic UI elements and human cognitive processes using algorithmic components (4) it allows interfacing with external data; (5) it supports modeling probabilistic models using mixed models; (6) it allows offline analysis of simulation results. In addition, this chapter presents a software prototype 'CogTool+' by extending the well-known cognitive modeling tool CogTool (John et al. Predictive human performance modeling made easy. In: Proceedings of the SIGCHI Conference on Human Factors in Computing Systems, CHI'04, pp 455–462. ACM, New York (2004). http://doi.acm.org/10.1145/985692.985750) (see Chap. 2) following the proposed framework (part of this chapter will appear in a full paper which is currently under review. (Yuan, H., Li, S., Rusconi, P., "*CogTool+: Modeling human performance at large scale*".)).

5.1 A New Conceptual Framework

This conceptual framework is designed to be flexible, re-configurable, and supporting automation of modeling and simulating human cognitive tasks. Inspired by the website design practice, where designers and programmers can efficiently work together on a large website project with clear task separation. Designers can use Cascading Style Sheets (CSS) or What You can See Is What You can Get (WYSIWYG) Hypertext Markup Language (HTML) editor to complete website UI design task, while programmers can use advanced HTML coding, JavaScript and/or server-side programming to complete back-end tasks to support designers. To achieve a similar level of compatibility and flexibility with existing practices of cognitive modeling, we propose the framework to have the following 5 features:

H. Yuan et al., *Cognitive Modeling for Automated Human Performance Evaluation at Scale*, Human–Computer Interaction Series,
https://doi.org/10.1007/978-3-030-45704-4_5

- to use a human- and machine-readable language to support high-level parameterization and automation.
- to have algorithmic components to support modeling dynamic UI and modeling dynamic human cognitive processes.
- to develop flexible interfaces to allow ingesting external data using algorithmic components to facilitate the modeling process.
- to include mixed models to model and capture the probabilistic nature of many human cognitive processes.
- to offer offline analysis processes to provide functionalities for data collection, data analysis and visualization.

This framework should be built by means of the common effort of psychologists, computer scientists, and programmers. Psychologists can provide data and knowledge to facilitate modeling process. Computer scientists/programmers can convert such information to reusable software modules/datasets to enrich the capabilities of the framework. With such arrangement, people working in different fields can relatively independently make contributions to support the framework.

As illustrated in Fig. 5.1, the framework consists of four main components: *Generator*, *Model Interpreter*, *Model Simulator*, and *Offline Analyzer*. Each main component can interface with external data. This makes the proposed framework more compatible and configurable, meaning that it has the flexibility to model data-driven modeling tasks.

Moreover, each blue rounded-corner rectangle represents a software module that can be customized, meaning that parts of the framework can be modified/replaced to meet designers/users' requirements. For instance, a system has a XML-based machine readable language, and the parser of model interpreter could be designed as a XML parser. If a system specialises on modeling CPM-GOMS models, the cognitive model simulator should be a CPM-GOMS-based simulator. Such inclusion of customizable software modules ensures that the proposed framework is featured with generalizability and reconfigurability.

Nevertheless, several parts of the framework require human involvements as shown in the figure, suggesting that the framework should have a number of GUIs/a general GUI to help users to complete modeling tasks.

In the rest of this section, we will explain each component with more details.

5.1.1 Generator

The main aim of a generator is to create meta models, where each meta model describes the system to be modeled in terms of its UI elements and how the users interact with the system (i.e., interaction workflows). Each meta model has two submodels: a descriptive model and an algorithmic model.

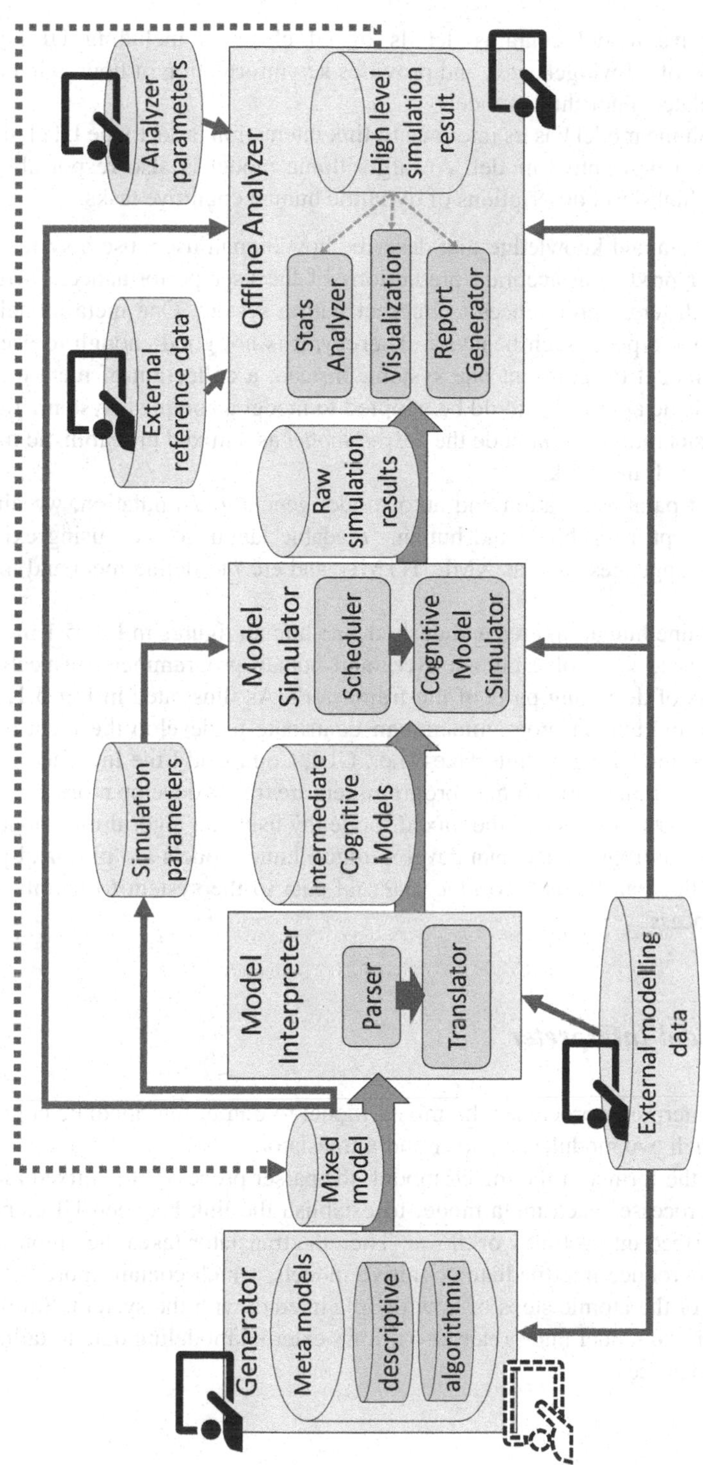

Fig. 5.1 Proposed system framework diagram

- A descriptive model contains details of UI elements including UI layout, description of UI widgets etc., and provides key information of how to interface with its related algorithmic model.
- An algorithmic model has its interface to link interaction tasks to the UI elements defined in a descriptive model. An algorithmic model is also responsible for providing high-level descriptions of dynamic human cognitive tasks.

Accurate data and knowledge that describe how human users use a system can be crucial for producing accurate predictions of the user performance. Different people have different preferences to interact with a system. One meta model can only define one type of such behavior. Thereby, it is not good enough to use one single meta model to represent one system. Instead, a collection of meta models with probabilistic approach should be adopted to model a complete system. Taking this into consideration, we include the *Mixed model* as a mixed probabilistic model to be part of the framework.

To support parameterization and auto model generation/simulation, we aim to develop or adopt a machine- and human- readable language (i.e., using existing standardized languages such as XML, HTML, and etc.) to define meta and mixed models.

The solid-line human figures and dashed-line human figures in Fig. 5.1 indicate that there is need to involve human users and human programmers, respectively, in the process of designing parts of the framework. As illustrated in Fig. 5.1, both human users and human programmers can contribute to develop the meta model and the mixed model via the interfaces (i.e., GUI, Command Line Interface (CLI)) provided by the framework. Human programmers are free to develop more advanced and complex meta models and the mixed model by using an algorithmic model. In addition, human programmers can develop algorithmic models as "plug-and-play" components that can be used to glue external data to the system to facilitate the modeling process.

5.1.2 Model Interpreter

The model interpreter processes the mixed model to output intermediate cognitive models through two modules: a parser and a translator.

Based on the format of the mixed model, the parser processes the mixed model, and it then processes each meta model to establish the link between UI elements and the described interaction workflows. Then the translator takes the output from the parser to produce intermediate cognitive models, which contain more detailed descriptions of the atomic steps of how people interact with the system. Similar to the generator, the model interpreter also allows external modeling data to tailor the interpretation process.

5.1.3 Model Simulator

The model simulator takes the intermediate cognitive models produced by the model interpreter as input, and use a scheduler and a cognitive model simulator to automate the modeling and simulation processes at a large scale.

A scheduler is used to arrange parallel computing (via GPU or multiple CPUs) tasks to accelerate the simulation process. After completion of the scheduled tasks, the cognitive model simulator initiates the simulation process with the input of simulation parameters, which are defined during the generation of the mixed model. The output of this process is a series of simulation results for all generated intermediate cognitive models.

5.1.4 Offline Analyzer

The offline analyzer provides a way to collect, analyze, and visualize simulation results interactively and collectively. It consists of three modules that further process the raw simulation results: (1) The stats analyzer module is responsible for conducting statistical analyses. The external reference data (i.e., data from real human experiments) can be used for deriving the statistical differences; (2) Users can use the visualization module to review the modeling and simulation results. It also allows users to customize the visualization parameters to review the results interactively; (3) Users can use the report generator to produce modeling reports by interfacing with additional inputs from the analyzer parameter, and/or the mixed model, and/or external reference data, and/or external modeling data.

5.2 CogTool+: A Prototype of a Software Implementation

To demonstrate the effectiveness and usefulness of the proposed conceptual framework, we implemented a software prototype CogTool+ (see Fig. 5.2) inspired by the open source software CogTool [4].

CogTool supports the use of the XML format to import and export its projects, which allows users to model cognitive tasks in a flexible and re-configurable approach. We decided to adopt and extend CogTool XML schema to help design and define high-level modeling tasks. This can offer a dynamic and scalable approach to support parameterization and automation of cognitive task modeling. In addition, this ensures that CogTool+ could be compatible with CogTool, and potentially contribute to the advancement of the CogTool research community.

The users of CogTool+ do not need to know the detailed psychological theoretical and empirical evidence underlying the elements that encompass a model. Similar to the HCI community's current approaches to integrating psychological data

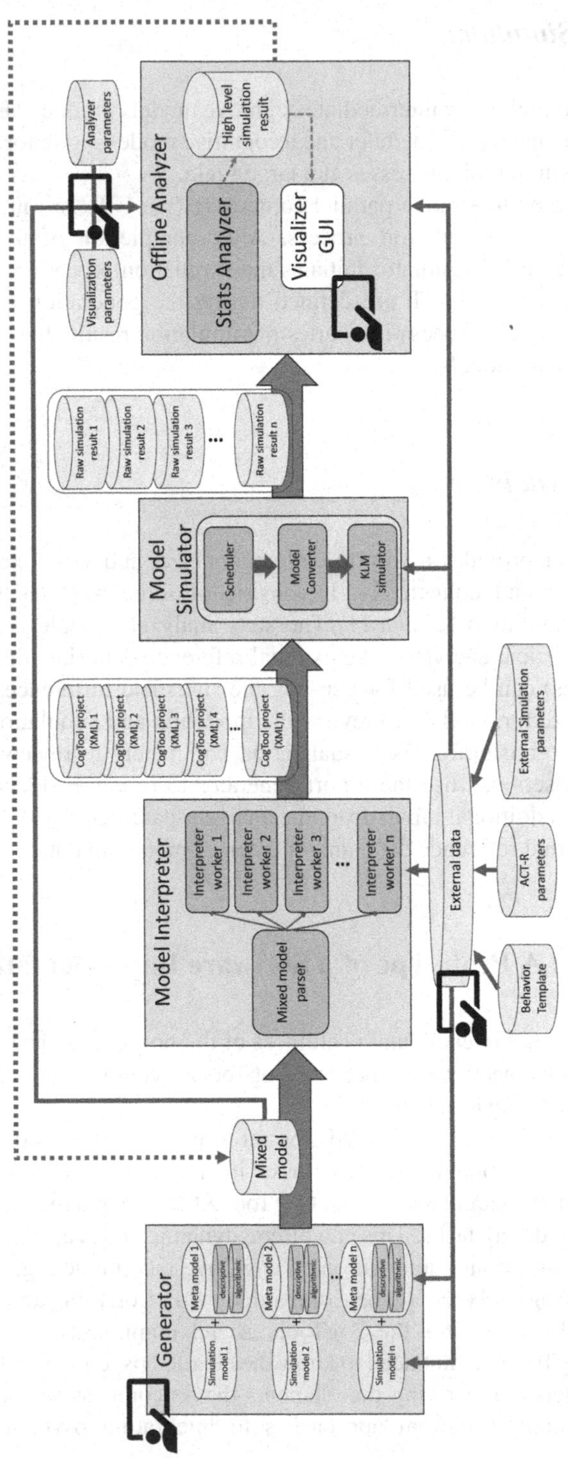

Fig. 5.2 System framework of CogTool+

into software tools/systems (e.g., see [1, 5]), the psychological evidence used in CogTool+ should be limited to the design level, which is obtained from the collaboration with psychologists or extracted from previous related studies. For the programming components of CogTool+, the user does not need to be proficient at programming, but only to be knowledgeable of existing software modules (produced by computer scientists and psychologists) by following user manuals such as referring to a random function for modeling dynamic UI elements.

CogTool's cognitive operators such as 'Think' and 'Homing' are compatible and supported by CogTool+. In addition, CogTool+ can interface with external data such as eye-tracking data, data extracted from Fitts's Law experiments, and data from previous related literature to better tailor the modeling process. Moreover, such data can be converted into algorithmic modules as part of the behavior templates/datasets generated by psychologists and computer programmers to better support UI/UX designers/practitioners to use this software.

5.2.1 Generator

The users of CogTool+ can use the generator to define the system UI and user-interaction tasks using the *Simulation model*, *Meta model*, and *Mixed model*. All three models are written in the XML format.

5.2.1.1 Simulation Model

One simulation model works with an associated meta model to define high-level parameters such as Fitts Law parameters, and also configure simulation settings to be used at a later stage of the modeling process. As illustrated in Fig. 5.3, a simulation model consists of the following three parts:

1. The first part declares the total number of simulations for a particular task.
2. The second one is to set the simulation parameters. As illustrated in the Fig. 5.3, it allows for either a dynamic preference setting or a static preference setting. For the static preference setting, users can set fixed values of 48 and 136 for the two coefficients of the Fitts Law [2] equation `<fitts_cof>` and `fitts_min` respectively. Alternatively, for the dynamic preference setting, the `<fitts_cof>` and `<fitts_min>` can be set as dynamic parameters by configuring `<type>` to be 'dynamic' (i.e., `<type>dynamic</type>`). This can produce distributions accordingly.

   By default, CogTool adds 1.2 s of thinking time automatically to the first 'demonstration' step/'Look-at' step. As illustrated in the Fig. 5.3, CogTool+ allows a user to set the `<imply_think></imply_think>` element as 'false' to disable this default behavior. This feature demonstrates that CogTool+ has the capability to update its parameters pro-grammatically and dynamically.

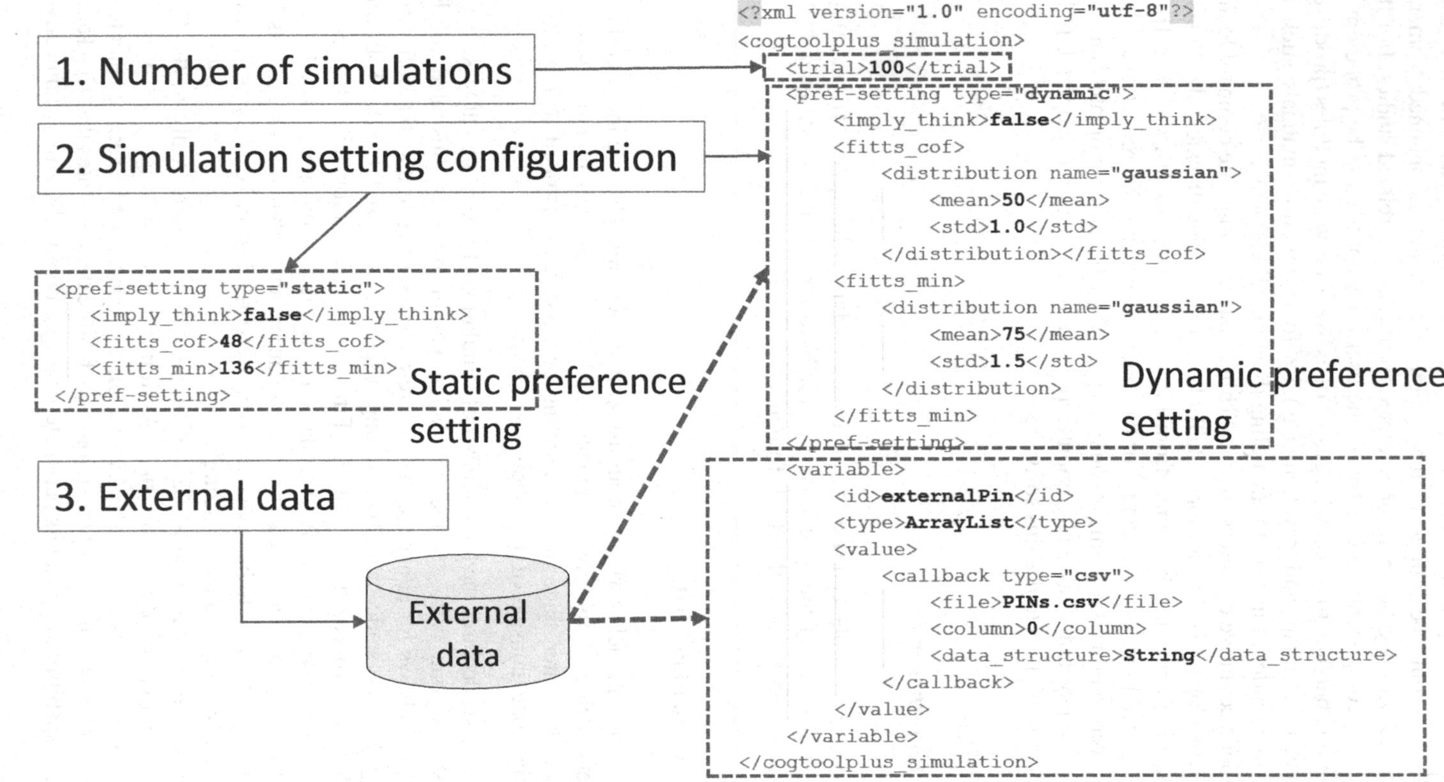

Fig. 5.3 An example of simulation models written in XML

In addition, users can design higher-level interaction workflows, and dynamically define parameters such as 'Think' and 'Look-at'. The CogTool+ system can automatically translate and convert the high-level description to a list of scripts that are equivalent to the 'Script Step List' produced using CogTool.

It should be noted that, such changes to the operators' execution time should be based on a joint decision of psychologists and programmers or based on empirical evidence from previous literature or empirical experiments.

3. The third one is to interface with external data that will be processed in a later stage. As illustrated in Fig. 5.3, external data saved in the CSV format can be added using `<variable>` element.

5.2.1.2 Meta Models

One meta model is used to define the high-level UIs of a system, and it also describes one particular behavior of how people interact with the system. As previously illustrated, a meta model has two components: a descriptive model and an algorithmic model.

Descriptive Models

A descriptive model defines the static parts of the UI including its layout, size, widgets etc. It also describes the interface that is used to integrate its associated algorithmic model. The descriptive model is written in the XML format, and it has five main elements. As shown in Fig. 5.4, each element has its own feature and its own child element/elements. It should be noted that, apart from the root element, the elements in light green define UI-related components, and the elements in light yellow describe user-interaction-related components.

Algorithmic Models

In our implementation of CogTool+, an algorithmic model can be written in JavaScript to support the parameterization and automation of human cognitive task modeling. A "plug-and-play" approach is adopted to integrate an algorithmic model with a descriptive model to offer users the freedom to interface with other external data as well as modeling dynamic UI elements and interaction workflows.

For instance, a JavaScript function can be designed to model dynamic user interactions as a dynamic interaction workflow instead of manually developing atomic action events one by one. To better model more complex conditional interactive tasks, the JavaScript functions can be designed as recursive and iterative functions to generate condition-based outputs. In addition to using JavaScript to design algorithmic models, the CSV format can also be used by users who have less experience with programming in JavaScript.

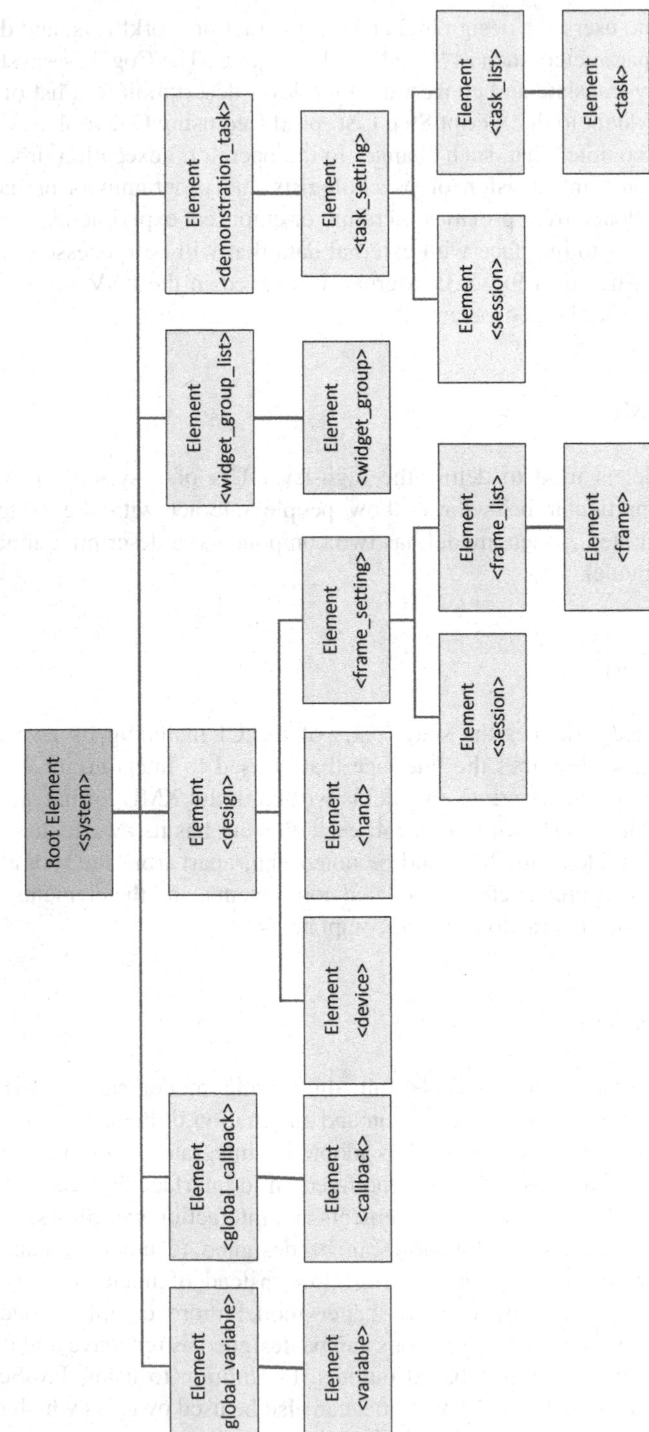

Fig. 5.4 The XML tree structure of a descriptive meta model

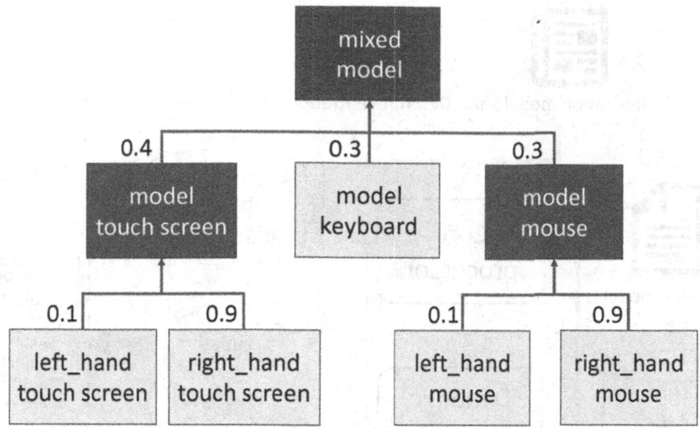

Fig. 5.5 The tree-like structure of an example of complex mixed models

5.2.1.3 Mixed Models

A mixed model represents a mixed-probabilistic model that consists of a number of meta models with their own probabilities. Here we present an example to better explain its concept and to demonstrate our implementation. Let us assume that the modeling task consists of making a prediction of the overall performance of a system that allows touch screen, keyboard, and mouse to be used as the input devices with the following criteria: (1) 90% of sampling population is right-handed and 10% is right handed for both mouse and touch screen users; (2) the percentages of using touch screen, keyboard, and mouse are 40%, 30%, and 30%, respectively.

To model this, the user needs to design individual meta models for each subset of users and a mixed model as shown in Fig. 5.5. A light green block in this figure represents one subset of users (i.e., one meta model), a dark green block represents a group of subsets of users (i.e., a sub-mixed model), and a blue block represents the whole sampling population (i.e., mixed model). To be noticed that a sub-mixed model can be formed by a number of meta models, or a number of sub-mixed models, or a mixture of meta models and sub-mixed model. The mixed model at the root node of the modeling tree (at the top level) has the same characteristics as one sub-mixed model.

5.2.2 Model Interpreter

The main task of the model interpreter is to take a mixed model as the input, and outputs a number of CogTool-compatible XML projects. The internal workflow of the model interpreter involves a mixed model parser and a number of interpreter workers. The mixed model parser is a customized XML parser that processes a mixed model, and that subsequently allocates a number of interpreter workers to

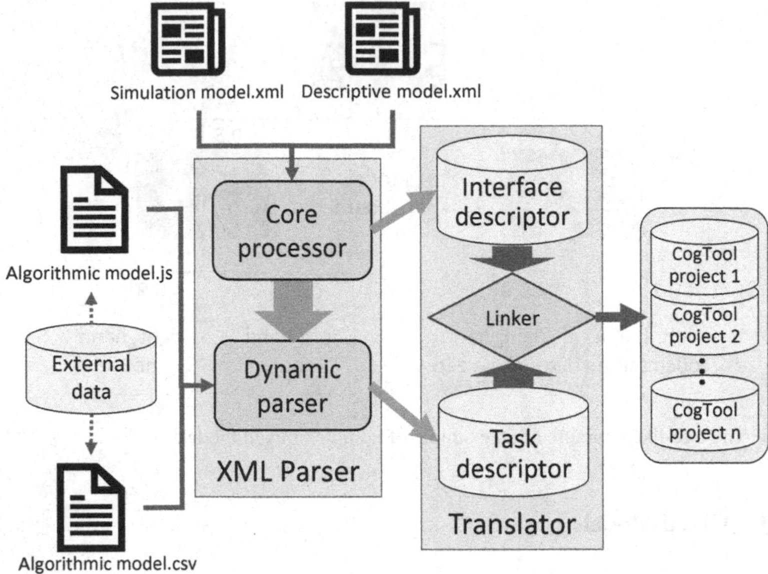

Fig. 5.6 The internal structure of the interpreter worker

process each individual meta model with its associated simulation model. The last task of the model interpreter is to generate a number of CogTool-compatible projects.

5.2.2.1 The Interpreter Worker

Figure 5.6 shows the internal structure of an interpreter worker, whereby each interpreter worker has a XML parser and a translator as demonstrated in Fig. 5.6.

The core processor of the XML parser is implemented in a similar way as the Document Object Model (DOM) XML parser. It takes the complete content of the descriptive model and simulation model as the input, and then it outputs an associated hierarchical tree in memory. Then the core processor classifies the hierarchical tree, and it separates the UI descriptions from the user-interaction descriptions. Lastly, the core processor redirects the UI descriptions and user-interaction descriptions to the interface descriptor and the dynamic parser, respectively.

The interface descriptor converts the high-level UI descriptions to low-level descriptions of UIs (i.e., UI layouts, size of widgets, position of widgets etc.). The dynamic parser interfaces with the algorithmic models written in both JavaScript and/or the CSV format to feed external data/functions into the processing pipeline. The dynamic parser sends the processed information to the task descriptor, which converts them to the atomic level interaction steps. Then the linker merges and processes both the low-level UI descriptions and the user-interaction descriptions

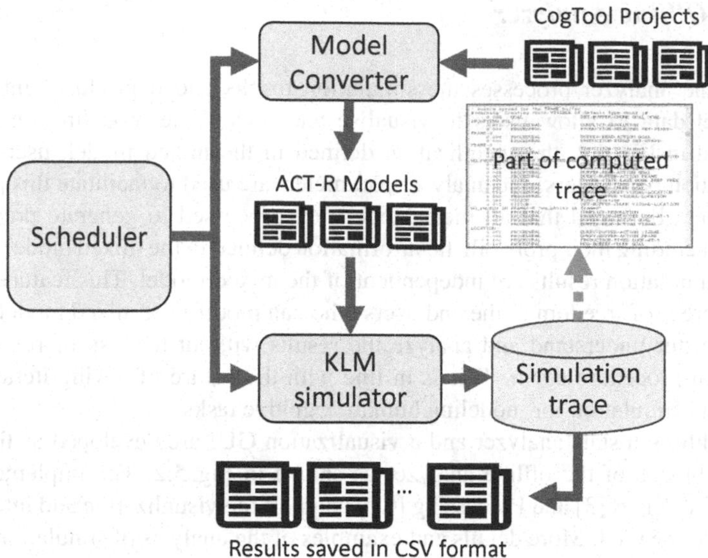

Fig. 5.7 The flowchart illustrating the working pipeline of the model simulator

to generate a number of CogTool projects. Each generated CogTool project is stored locally for an easy validation and an easy independent review if required.

5.2.3 Model Simulator

Compiling computer simulations and collecting user performance predictions are the main tasks of a model simulator. Figure 5.7 demonstrates the internal working pipeline of the model simulator. The scheduler is used to arrange the processing order.[1] The ordering information is then sent to the model converter and KLM simulator. CogTool projects generated by the model interpreter are processed and converted into a number of ACT-R models by the model converter using CogTool's back-end ACT-R framework. Next, the converted ACT-R models are parsed by the KLM simulator to generate the simulation trace, which contains details of completion time such as overall completion time for the whole task, time per cognition operator, time per vision etc. All these results are converted into the CSV format and stored locally.

[1]The current version of CogTool+ only supports sequential CPU processing. Parallel CPU/GPU processing will be implemented in a future version.

5.2.4 *Offline Analyzer*

The offline analyzer processes the simulation results and it produces interactive high-level data to allow users to visualise and review the modeling results. As illustrated in Fig. 5.2, the specification defined in the mixed model, user-defined visualization parameters, and analyzer parameters are used to facilitate this process.

It should be noted that all meta models are processed to generate predictions without including their probabilistic information defined in the mixed model. Hence, the raw simulation results are independent of the mixed model. This features offers some degrees of freedom to the end users who can modify the mixed model in run-time to better understand and analyze the results without the risk of running the simulation procedure again. This is in line with the nature of having iterations of design and simulation for modeling human cognitive tasks.

In addition, a stats analyzer and a visualization GUI are developed as the main building blocks of the offline analyzer as shown in Fig. 5.2. The implementation adopts JFreeChart [3] and Processing [6] to support the visualization and interaction features of the GUI. More details and examples of the analysis of simulation results are reported in Chap. 6.

5.2.5 *External Data*

One key feature of the proposed framework mentioned in Sect. 5.1 and of CogTool+ is to support the interface with external data to facilitate the modeling and simulation processes. This is mainly achieved by incorporating JavaScript and the CSV format as parts of the algorithmic model.

CogTool+ currently supports the interface with behavior template databases, ACT-R parameters, and external simulation parameters. Our previous work [7] revealed that human-behavior patterns extracted from eye-tracking data can help shape the human cognitive modeling tasks. Such information and knowledge could be converted as reusable behavior template databases as a part of CogTool+.

We have implemented some behavior template databases written in JavaScript based on results obtained in previous research as well as from manual analysis of empirical studies. Nevertheless, we are planing to develop automatic approaches to extract and generate behavior template databases from human behavioral datasets such as eye-tracking and EEG data.

In addition, CogTool+ allows users to interface with external data sources to edit some parameters that are originally set with fixed values in CogTool. This can provide users with the flexibility to define and model human cognitive tasks. For instance, Fitts's Law parameters can be empirically determined and then used for modeling tasks. Moreover, as mentioned above, external simulation parameters can be added to the *Offline Analyzer* to enrich the data visualization capabilities of CogTool+. More details about the interface with external data can be found in Chap. 6.

References

1. Anderson, J.: How Can the Human Mind Occur in the Physical Universe? Oxford University Press, Oxford (2007)
2. Fitts, P.: The information capacity of the human motor system in controlling the amplitude of movement. J. Exp. Psychol. **47**(6), 381–391 (1954)
3. Gilbert, D.: JFreeChart: a free 100% Java chart library (2015). http://www.jfree.org/jfreechart/. Accessed 07 Feb 2018
4. John, B., Prevas, K., Salvucci, D., Koedinger, K.: Predictive human performance modeling made easy. In: Proceedings of the SIGCHI Conference on Human Factors in Computing Systems, CHI'04, pp. 455–462. ACM, New York (2004). http://doi.acm.org/10.1145/985692.985750
5. Laird, J.: The Soar Cognitive Architecture. MIT Press, London (2012)
6. Reas, C., Fry, B.: Processing: programming for the media arts. AI Soc. Knowl. Cult. Commun. **20**(4), 526–538 (2006)
7. Yuan, H., Li, S., Rusconi, P., Aljaffan, N.: When eye-tracking meets cognitive modeling: applications to cyber security systems. In: Human Aspects of Information Security, Privacy and Trust: 5th International Conference, HAS 2017, Held as Part of HCI International 2017, Vancouver, 9–14 July 2017, Proceedings. Lecture Notes in Computer Science, vol. 10292, pp. 251–264. Springer, Cham (2017)

Chapter 6
Example Applications of CogTool+

Abstract In this chapter, we demonstrate and evaluate the effectiveness and usefulness of the developed software prototype CogTool+. In particular, we present our work of using CogTool+ to model three existing systems. The first system is an observer-resistant password system called Undercover; the second one is a 6-digit PIN entry system, and the third one is data entry interfaces (part of this chapter will appear in a full paper which is currently under review. (Yuan, H., Li, S., Rusconi, P., "*CogTool+: Modeling human performance at large scale*".))

6.1 Modeling the User Authentication System Undercover

Undercover [4] is an observer-resistant password system developed based on the theory of partially-observable challenges. More details of Undercover can be found in Chap. 4, Sect. 4.2.2.

The selection of Undercover for the evaluation of CogTool+ has the following reasons:

1. As a relative complex system, Undercover involves a number of dynamic cognitive tasks. To accurately capture them, it will require to model static UIs with dynamic user interactions.
2. We would like to prove that it is easier to model such complex system by utilizing the parameterization and automation features of CogTool+.
3. We would like to compare the predicted data using CogTool+ with the data obtained from a lab-based user study [3] to evaluate CogTool+.

6.1.1 Modeling with CogTool+

In order to make a direct comparison with the findings reported by Perković [3], CogTool+ is used to model their implementation of Undercover as illustrated in Fig. 4.1c in Chap. 4, Sect. 4.2.2. One of the main findings from their study reveals

H. Yuan et al., *Cognitive Modeling for Automated Human Performance Evaluation at Scale*, Human–Computer Interaction Series,
https://doi.org/10.1007/978-3-030-45704-4_6

that the non-uniform human behaviors can indicate potential security problems in using Undercover.

We would like to find out if CogTool+ can automatically identify such insecure behaviors. Firstly, we need to establish the understanding of how the system works using a descriptive model and an algorithmic model.

6.1.1.1 Designing a Descriptive Model

Firstly, each user needs to choose 5 'pass-pictures', and then complete 7 challenge screens, whereby each challenge screen has the same UI as shown in Fig. 4.1c in Chap. 4, Sect. 4.2.2. The UI of a challenge screen is treated as one static element to be modeled using a descriptive model. 7 challenge screens can be automatically produced using a descriptive model as illustrated in Fig. 6.1. Then the Undercover UI as represented in Fig. 6.1a is converted into the high-level description of UI as shown in Fig. 6.1b using XML.

Next, a global variable is defined in the descriptive model to indicate the number of challenge screens (i.e., `<global_variable>` as highlighted in the red rectangle). The attribute 'type' of `<frame_setting>` is set to be 'dynamic'. Based on the above setting, the model interpreter can automatically generate the detailed descriptions of the 7 challenge screens as shown in Fig. 6.1(c).

6.1.1.2 Designing an Algorithmic Model

To model the dynamic elements of the Undercover system (i.e., how people complete the authentication task) using an algorithmic model is more complex as there is a number of micro-tasks requiring dynamic inputs/outputs. Hence we dissected the whole authentication session into the following tasks:

1. Task 1 Password selection: the user needs to select 5 'pass-pictures' from 28 pictures.
2. Task 2 Challenge screens arrangement: each of 5 out of 7 challenge screens needs to contain one unique 'pass-picture'. Each of the other 2 challenge screens needs to have one 'no pass-picture'. The arrangement of the decoy pictures should ensure that they are different for each challenge screen.
3. Task 3 Position of the 'pass-picture' for each challenge screen: the position of the 'pass-picture' or 'no pass-picture' can be derived by using the arrangement of pictures displayed for each challenge screen (i.e., this is known from task 2) and the selected password (i.e., this is known from task 1).
4. Task 4 Random hidden challenge for each challenge screen: the system needs to generate a random hidden challenge (i.e., one value from: 'Up', 'Down', 'Left', 'Right', 'Center').
5. Task 5 Public response for each challenge screen: the specific layout corresponding to the generated hidden challenge can be derived using the hidden challenge

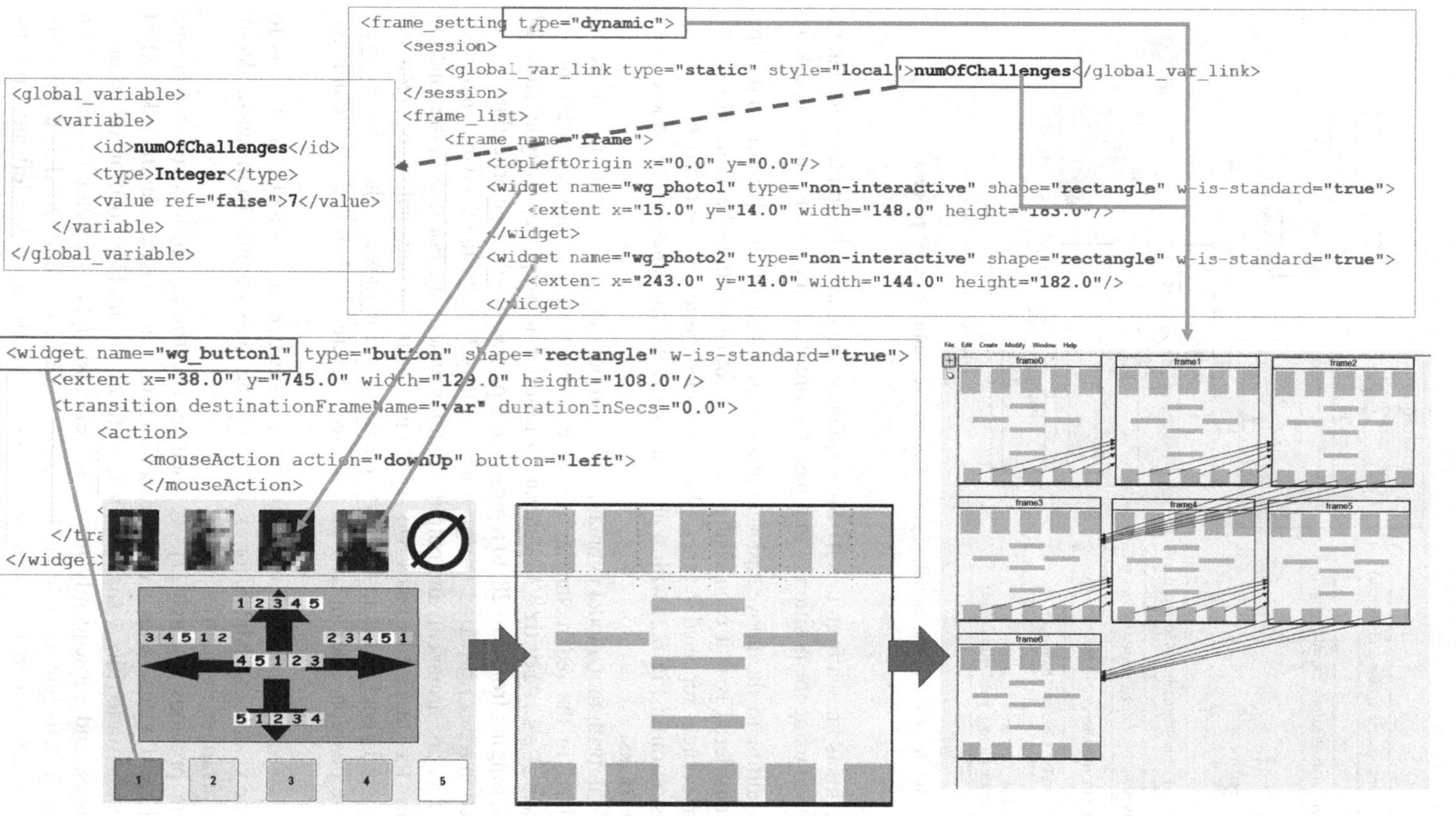

Fig. 6.1 Modeling the creation of 7 challenge screens: **(a)** Undercover UI; **(b)** Visualization of Undercover UI model for 1 challenge screen; **(c)** Visualization of Undercover UI models for 7 challenge screens

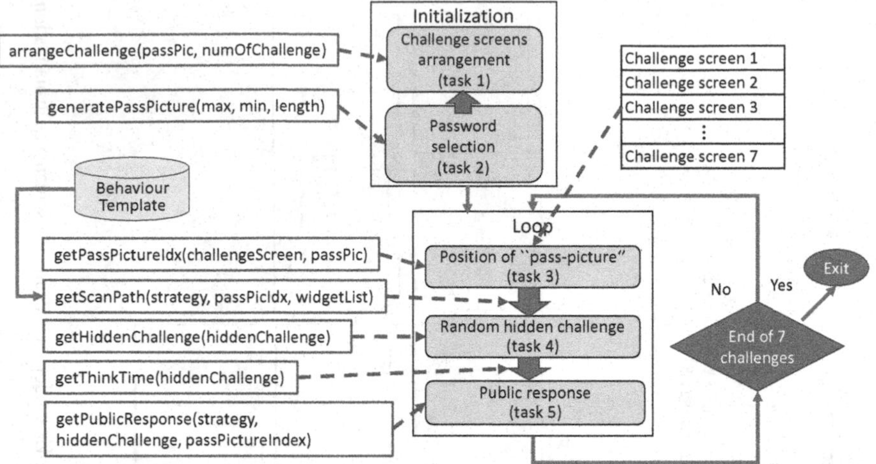

Fig. 6.2 The flowchart of the modeling of the Undercover authentication process

(i.e., this is known from task 4). Subsequently, the correct button to press can be obtained using the position of the 'pass-picture' (i.e., this is known from task 3).

In addition to the above tasks, another dimension of the dynamic modeling to be considered is that each challenge screen must contain the same tasks with different content repeated 7 times. We developed an algorithmic model (i.e., see the illustration in Fig. 6.2) with a number of JavaScript functions to handle these dynamic tasks.

The algorithmic model contains a number of JavaScript functions as highlighted in the red rectangles in Fig. 6.2. First, task 1 utilizes the function `generatePassPicture` to generate 5 random non-repeated integers from 28 integers, ranging from 1 to 28, to represent the password selection procedure. Then, the function `arrangeChallenge` is used in task 2 to take the password generated in task 1 as one argument, and output 7 challenge screens. For task 3, the function `getPassPictureIdx` takes two arguments including one challenge screen and the password generated in task 1 to derive the position index of the 'pass-picture', or get the position index in case the 'no pass-picture' is identified for a challenge screen.

There is one important modeling task in-between task 3 and task 4. It is to model the visual-search behavior of searching the 'pass-picture' from several decoy pictures arranged in an array.

In our previous research [7], we used an eye tracker to discover that people had different visual scan paths for completing such visual-search tasks. Most participants started the visual-search task from the middle position of an array of pictures, and subsequently moved to left and right. We refer to this pattern as a centre-left-right visual-search strategy. We also identified that a minority of participants started the visual-search task directly from the left-most picture and ended the search process at the right-most picture. We refer to this pattern as left-right visual-search strategy. As shown in Fig. 6.2, `getScanPath` is a JavaScript function to integrate such visual-search behavior template/database with the algorithmic model to facilitate the modeling process.

`getHiddenChallenge` is a JavaScript function to generate a random number from 1 to 5 (i.e., 1 to 5 were used to represent five values of hidden challenges) as the hidden challenge index. Finally, the function `getPublicResponse` takes two arguments. One is the hidden challenge index, and another one is the 'pass-picture' position index. The output of the function `getPublicResponse` is the public challenge response, which indicates the button that needs to be pressed for *Task 5*.

We would like to point out that the mental effort to derive the public response needs to be considered in the design of the algorithmic model. Each hidden challenge button layout panel as depicted in Fig. 4.1b represents one unique hidden challenge index. The different orders of buttons in the different hidden challenge button layout panels could affect the reaction time and subsequently affect the predicted completion time.

For instance, the order of buttons of the hidden challenge button layout panel for the 'Up' hidden challenge is the same as the order of buttons for the response button panel (i.e., the order of button from left to right is 1, 2, 3, 4, 5). The assumption here could be that no or minimum effort is need to work out the public challenge response for the 'Up' hidden challenge. By contrast, the hidden challenge button layout panels for other hidden challenges have completely different order of buttons as shown in Fig. 4.1b, compared with the public response button panel. For these cases, it is possible that some level of mental effort is needed to work out the public response.

Keeping this in mind, we considered other cases except for the 'Up' hidden challenge as a single visual target search task. Based on previous research [5, 6], there is a linear relationship between reaction time and the number of images (i.e., windows size as mentioned in [5, 6]). We can use the formula $rt = 0.583 + 0.0529.w$ [6], where w is the number of images, to estimate reaction time. Hence, given a hidden challenge (i.e., 'Left', 'Right', 'Centre', and 'Down'), `getThinkTime` is a JavaScript function to incorporate this information to dynamically derive the reaction time occurred between *Task 4* and *Task 5*.

Furthermore, researchers [7] also discovered that participants would normally visually confirm the position of the 'pass-picture' before completing the authentication task. We refer to this process as 'confirmation process' for the rest of this chapter. To integrate this observed behavior, another 'Look-at' action is added to the 'pass-picture' position before pressing the button for *Task 5* if the 'confirmation process' is presented for the modeling task.

6.1.1.3 Designing a Mixed Model

The last step is to design a mixed model. As we have witnessed different behavior patterns in a previous study [7], we developed a number of individual meta models to represent them.[1]

[1]Based on these behavior patterns, we developed reusable JavaScript-based behavior template database patterns as part of the CogTool+ software.

These individual meta models are CLR-Only (center-left-right without confirmation process), LR-Only (left-right without confirmation process), CLR-Confirm (center-left-right with confirmation process), and LR-Confirm (left-right with confirmation process). Next, different weights were assigned to the different meta models. In addition, we developed one associated simulation model for each meta model, whereby each simulation model was configured to compile 150 simulation trials and generate 150 predictions.

In summary, 150 (simulations) $\times$ 4 (individual meta models) $=$ 600 predictions will be generated for this experiment. We would like to emphasize that all meta models work with the same simulation setting and algorithmic model, and thereby we only need to design and develop one simulation model and one algorithmic model for the whole experiment.

6.1.1.4 Results

For this modeling task, we would like to know if CogTool+ can produce the predicted average response time for each hidden challenge value similar to the findings identified in the previous lab-based user study [3]. In their study, real human users had fastest response time for the 'Up' hidden challenge. CogTool+ produced similar results as depicted in Fig. 6.3, where Fig. 6.3a is the screenshot of the actual figure generated using the CogTool+ visualization feature, and Fig. 6.3b is the actual figure of the real human data obtained from the paper [3]. In addition, another behavioral pattern is identified in our study: the response time is slowest in the absence of the pass picture (see Fig. 6.4).

Inherited from CogTool, the estimation of user performance using CogTool+ is for skilled users. However, the user performance data [3] were from relatively unskilled individuals. Thus, we did not make assumptions that the estimated results can match the findings from the real human user study reported in [3] exactly. Furthermore, the experiment settings are different. For example, there were two groups of participants in [3]. Participants from one group were instructed to use the mouse to complete the Undercover authentication tasks, whilst participants from another group were told to use the keyboard to complete the task. Hence, we anticipated that there will be some mismatch in the results.

One of the main findings from [3] was that researchers can investigate human behaviors (i.e., the non-uniform distribution of response time) to reveal system security issues. For this experiment, our intention was to find out if we can use CogTool+ to model the Undercover system and discover such non-uniform time distribution. We did not intend to make a direct comparison with the findings identified in [3]. The simulation results using CogTool+ indicates that the non-uniform patterns can be identified using CogTool+ even without considering the participants' skill level. The latter could explain the outstanding differences between the real user data and the predicted results.

In summary, these are the advantages of using CogTool+ to model Undercover:

1. It is relatively easier to model the dynamic elements of Undercover (e.g., selection of pass pictures, the pass picture and decoy pictures arrangement for the pub-

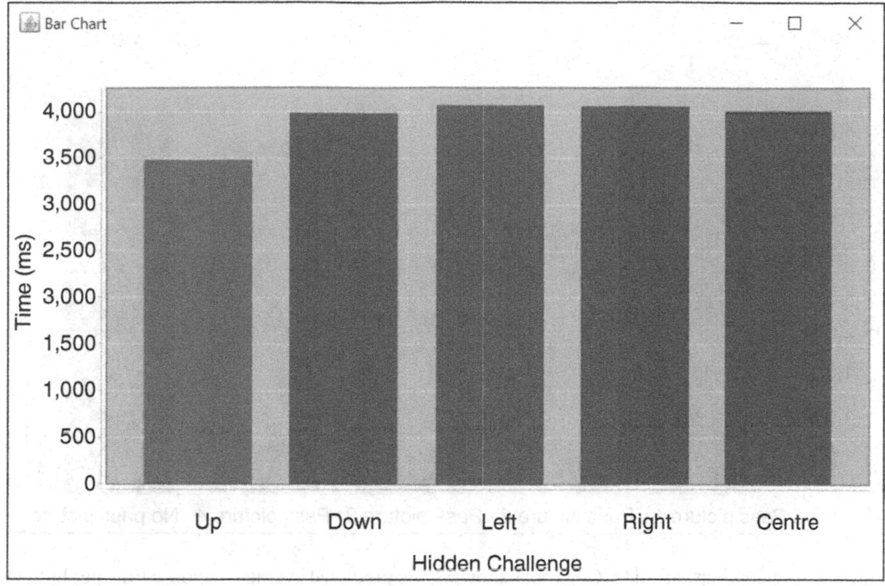

(a)

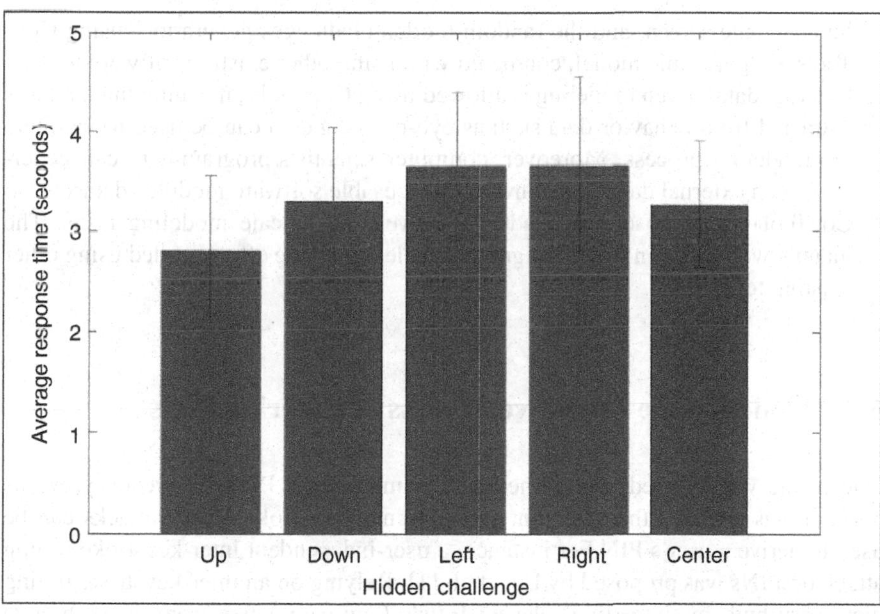

(b)

Fig. 6.3 (**a**) Bar chart produced by CogTool+ showing the predicted average response time per hidden challenge c_h using CogTool+; (**b**) Average response time per hidden challenge c_h using real human data (the error bars represent standard deviations) [3]

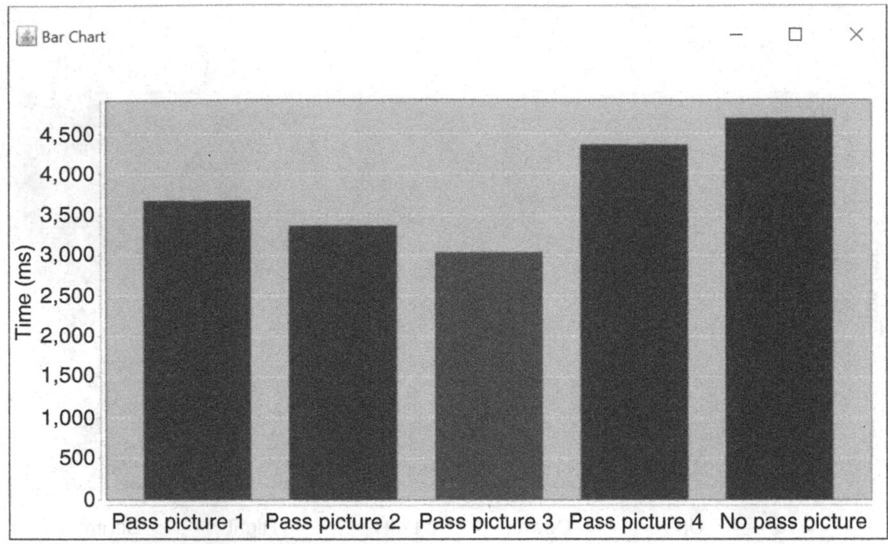

Fig. 6.4 Bar chart produced by CogTool+ showing the predicted average response time per hidden response r_h (i.e., pass picture position)

lic challenge screen, and the random hidden challenges generation) using CogTool+'s algorithmic model, compared with using other existing software tools.

2. External data-driven modeling is allowed using CogTool+, meaning that patterns extracted from behavior data such as eye-tracking data can be used to facilitate the modeling process. Moreover, computer scientists/programmers can generalise such external data, and convert it to reusable software modules/datasets.
3. CogTool+ allows users to conduct relatively large-scale modeling tasks. The manual work/effort needed is significantly less than the effort needed using other existing tools.

6.2 Modeling the Cognitive Process of Entering PINs

One of the widely used user authentication methods is PINs. However, previous research has revealed that different types of inter-keystroke timing attacks can be used to derive a user's PIN.For instance, a user-independent inter-keystroke timing attack on PINs was proposed by Liu et al. [1]. Relying on an inter-keystroke timing dictionary built by extracting relevant Fitts's Law parameters from a real human user study, the performance of this attack is believed to be significantly better than random guessing attacks.

Here, we would like to use CogTool+ to model large-scale 6-digit PIN entry tasks to make a comparison with the inter-keystroke data obtained from their study [1] to demonstrate that our approach is cost-effective and accurate.

Table 6.1 Examples of inter-keystroke timing sequences for PIN entry tasks

PIN	k1-k2	k2-k3	k3-k4	k4-k5	k5-k6	k6-enter
777777	202.2	204.0	207.9	204.1	212.8	320.2
603294	241.2	227.4	203.4	239.8	233.1	292.2

6.2.1 Modeling PIN Entry Using CogTool+

The real human user study [1] used 50 different 6-digit PINs. Participants of the user study were instructed to enter each PIN using the number pad as shown in Fig. 6.5a.

The goal of this study is to make a direct comparison between the inter-keystroke timing sequences generated using CogTool+ and the real human user data obtained by [1].

Each row in Table 6.1 represents one timing sequence of entering one PIN, whereby 6 timing intervals are recorded for one PIN. For example, each value under column 'k1-k2' represents the time interval between pressing the first digit and the second digit of a PIN, and each value under column 'k6-enter' is the time between pressing the last digit of a PIN and the <Enter> key.

Here, we present more details of modeling one 6-digit PIN entry task using CogTool+. As shown in Fig. 6.5, three major steps are needed to model one PIN entry task.

1. We developed a simulation model to interface with the external 50 PINs[2] saved in the CSV format via a `<callback>` function as highlighted in Fig. 6.5. A simulation variable with the ID of 'externalPin' as highlighted in red in the figure is created to store all PINs in memory. The descriptive model can refer to these 50 PINs using the 'externalPin' ID later as shown by the dashed arrows linking Step 1 and Step 3 in the Fig. 6.5.
2. We designed a descriptive model to define the UI of the number-pad (i.e., Fig. 6.5a), and translate it into its associated high-level description (i.e., Fig. 6.5b). The red rectangles linked with green arrows illustrate the use of `<widget>` to describe UI element 'slash' and 'minus' button.
3. In this step, the simulation model automatically assigns one PIN to the descriptive model. This PIN is defined as a `<global_variable` with ID of 'password' as highlighted in the red rectangle. Then, the descriptive model automatically produces a series of interaction events (i.e., pressing button) based on the PIN number. Another `<global_variable>` defined in the descriptive model is the 'numberFrame' as highlighted in the red rectangle. With its 'dynamic' attribute 'type' of `<frame_setting>`, the model interpreter is able to automatically generate more detailed descriptions of 7 frames as depicted in Fig. 6.5c.

The above three-step process is automatically executed until all modeling tasks are completed. It should be noted that, as this experiment does not need to consider probabilistic analysis for all PINs, the mixed model consists of only one meta model with the weight of 1.

[2]More information of 50 PINs used in this study can be found in [1].

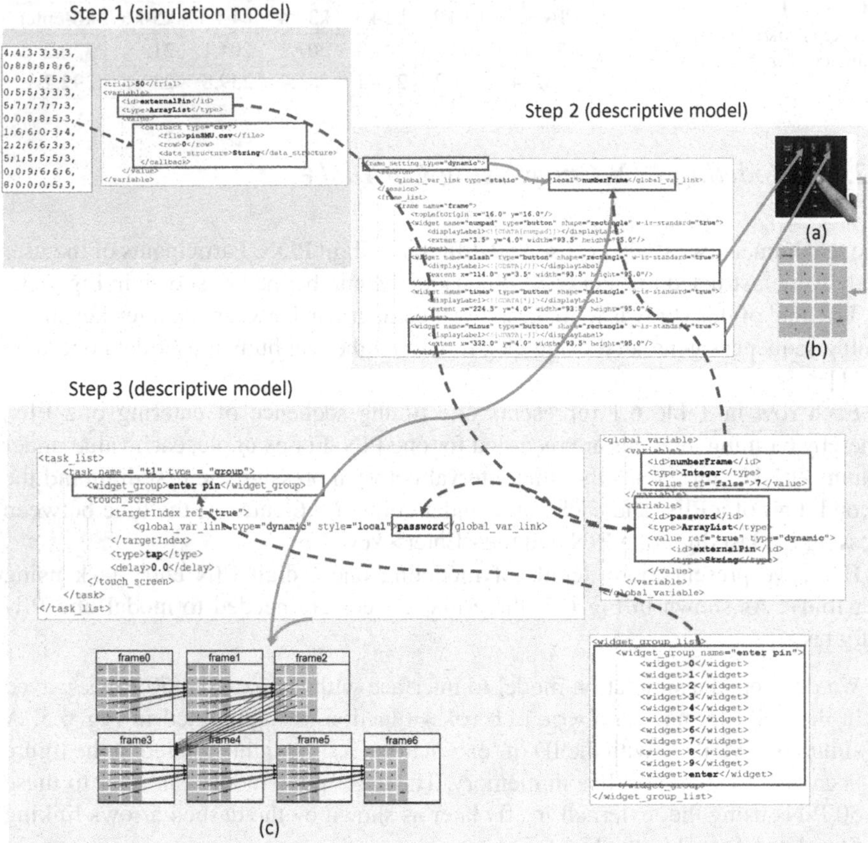

Fig. 6.5 Modeling one 6-digit PIN task: (**a**) PIN pad UI, (**b**) visualization of the PIN pad UI model, (**c**) visualization of entering one 6-digit PIN and press <Enter>

6.2.2 Results

The mean value of inter-keystroke timing sequences from the user study [1] was used for a comparison with the simulated data predicted using CogTool+. For a number of selected PINs, the differences between human data and simulated data are shown in Figs. 6.6 and 6.7. The correlation coefficients for PIN 000533 (see Fig. 6.6a), PIN 100086 (see Fig. 6.6b), PIN 990872 (see Fig. 6.7a), and PIN 443333 (see Fig. 6.7b) are 0.99096, 0.989956, 0.94458, and 0.97311, respectively. Moreover, the mean correlation coefficient for all PINs is 0.807, and the standard deviation of the correlation coefficients for all PINs is 0.233. This suggests that there is a strong association between the two datasets.

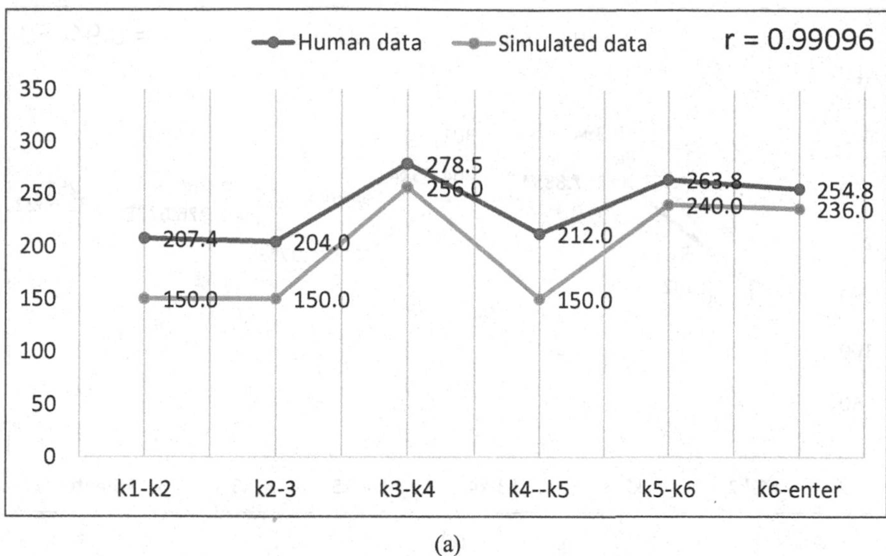

(a)

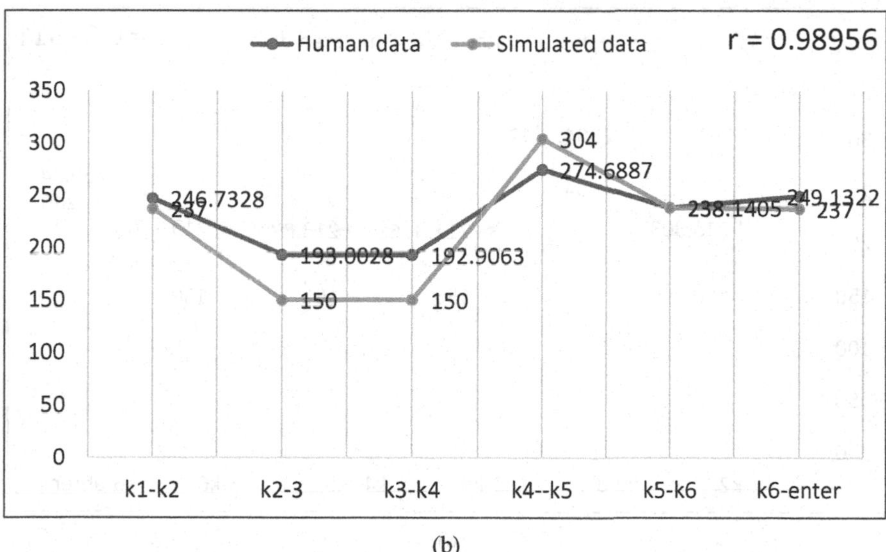

(b)

Fig. 6.6 Comparison of inter-keystroke timing data between human users and simulation, where y-axis is the performance time in milliseconds, and x-axis is the inter-keystroke time interval, *r* represents the correlation coefficient between the human data and the simulated data. (**a**) Inter-keystroke timing data for PIN 000533 (**b**) Inter-keystroke timing data for PIN 100086

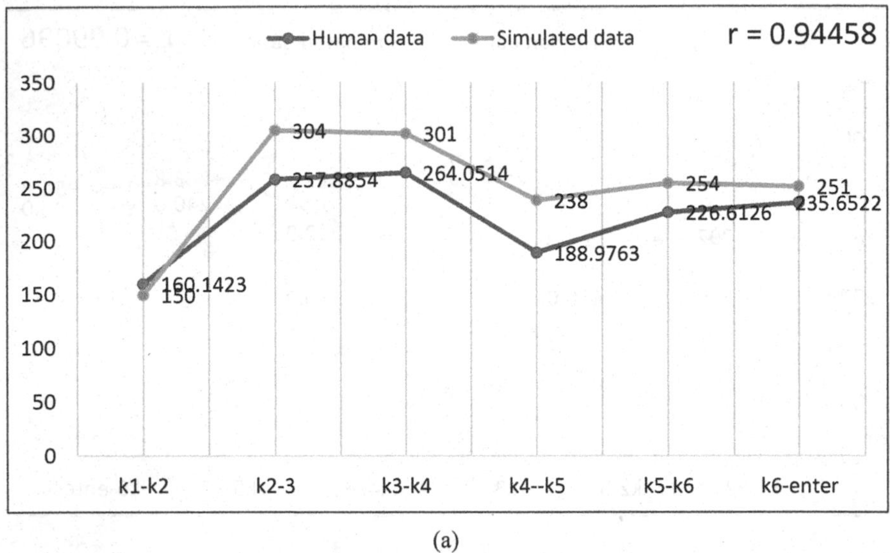

(a)

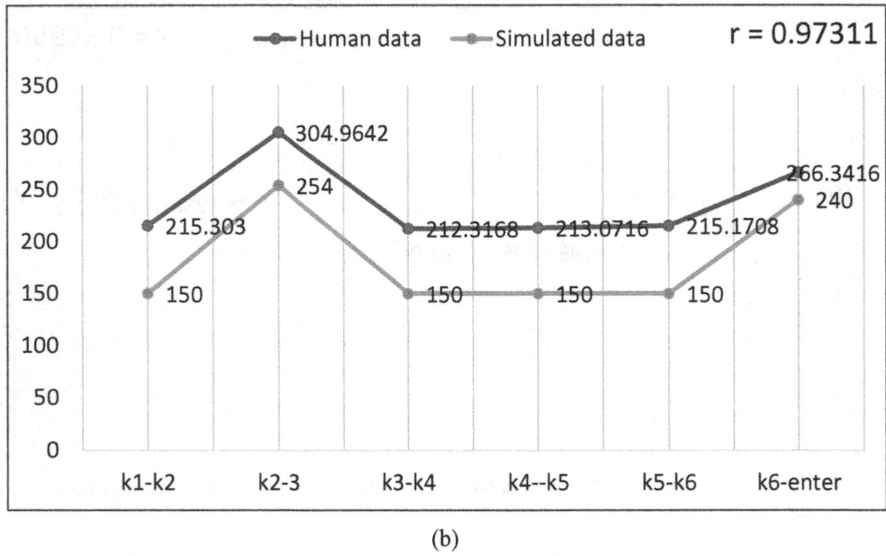

(b)

Fig. 6.7 Comparison of inter-keystroke timing data between human users and simulation, where y-axis is the performance time in milliseconds, and x-axis is the inter-keystroke time interval, r represents the correlation coefficient between the human data and the simulated data. (**a**) Inter-keystroke timing data for PIN 990872 (**b**) Inter-keystroke timing data for PIN 443333

6.3 Modeling Number Entry Interfaces

Number entry is an ubiquitous task, and different number entry interfaces have been designed. Among all, the numeric keypad is one of the most popular interfaces. A study was conducted to review number entry interfaces [2] for medical devices used for controlled drug delivery, and results suggested that interface style has a significant effect on speed and accuracy. In their study, participants performed fastest for Number pad (see Fig. 6.8a) and Up-down (see Fig. 6.8b) interfaces. Also, the interface preference score indicated that participants preferred the Number pad and Up-down interfaces. In this section, we would like to further demonstrate the effectiveness of CogTool+ by modeling these two number entry interfaces using CogTool+. Before going to the modeling details, a brief description of the two interfaces is presented.

6.3.1 *Number Pad*

Number pad interface uses a 12-key numeric keypad in the telephone style layout. The modeling process for number pad using CogTool+ is similar to the modeling task for the 6-digit PIN entry task mentioned in Sect. 6.2, and thus we will not describe the modeling details in this section, but only report the findings in comparison with the results obtained for modeling the Up-down interface.

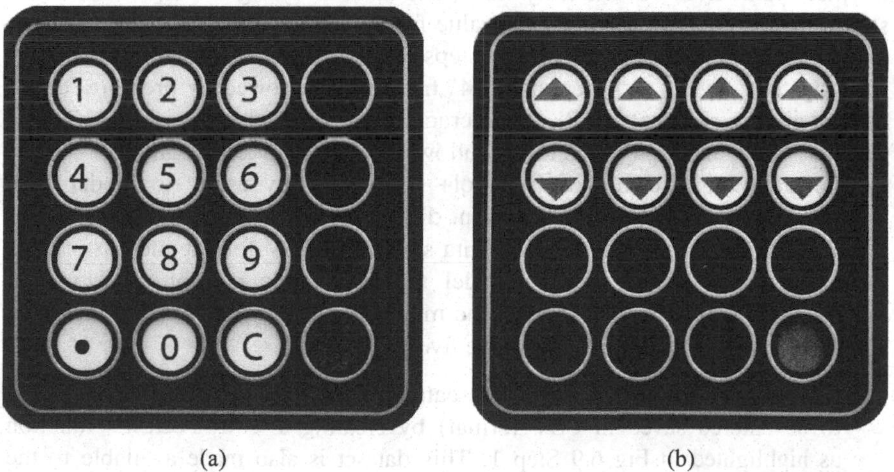

Fig. 6.8 Illustration of the number entry interfaces used in this study. (**a**) Illustration of Number pad interface [2] (**b**) Illustration of Up-down interface [2]

6.3.2 *Up-Down*

As illustrated in Fig. 6.8b, the Up-down interface consists of two rows of buttons. Buttons in the top row were used to increase the number, and buttons in the bottom row were used to decrease the number. Buttons are organized in four columns so that each column corresponds to a place value in the number. The left-most column represent tens digit, and the right-most column represents the hundredth place value. For the convenience and consistence, we will use the following references for these buttons for the rest of this section: 'up1', 'up2', 'up3', and 'up4' represent the first, second, third, and fourth button at the top row, respectively; 'down1', 'down2', 'down3', and 'down4' represent the first, second, third, and fourth button, respectively, at the bottom row.

6.3.2.1 Modeling Up-Down Number Entry Interface with CogTool+

The Up-down number entry interface seems straightforward to model. However, the interaction steps are dynamically determined by the entry number, and there are different ways to enter the same number. Hence, we would have to make following assumptions for convenience and consistency: (1) the interface starts with all zeros place values; (2) the number entry task starts from left to right, which is similar to the way we read a number; (3) we would like to consider the shortest path to complete the task taking into account that we are modeling skilled users. Hence, the assumption is that if a entry value is less than 5, the shortest path is to increase the place value from 0 to the entry value, and if the entry digit is larger than 5, the shortest path is to decrease the place value from 0 to the entry value. For instance: given a number '1.25', the interaction steps should consist of pressing 'up2' once, pressing 'up3' twice, and pressing 'up4' five times, followed by pressing 'enter' button; given a number '10.83', the interaction steps include pressing 'up1' once, 'down3' twice, and 'up4' three times, followed by pressing 'enter' button.

The algorithmic feature of CogTool+ could be very useful to model such relatively complicated tasks. In addition, differently from the examples presented in Sects. 6.1.1 and 6.2, both external data sources in CSV format and customized JavaScript functions are used to model the algorithmic part of the Up-down interface. We present more details of the modeling entering one number using the Up-down interface in Fig. 6.9. There are five major steps.

(1) In step 1, a simulation model is created to link external data (i.e., numbers to be entered saved in CSV format) by creating a `<callback>` function as highlighted in Fig. 6.9 Step 1. This dataset is also made available to the descriptive model as a simulation variable with the ID of 'numberEntry' (highlighted in red).
(2) In step 2, we define some global variables at the beginning of the descriptive model. As illustrated in Fig. 6.9 step 2, a `variable` with ID of 'number' is defined, and the value of this variable is a number from the external CSV file.

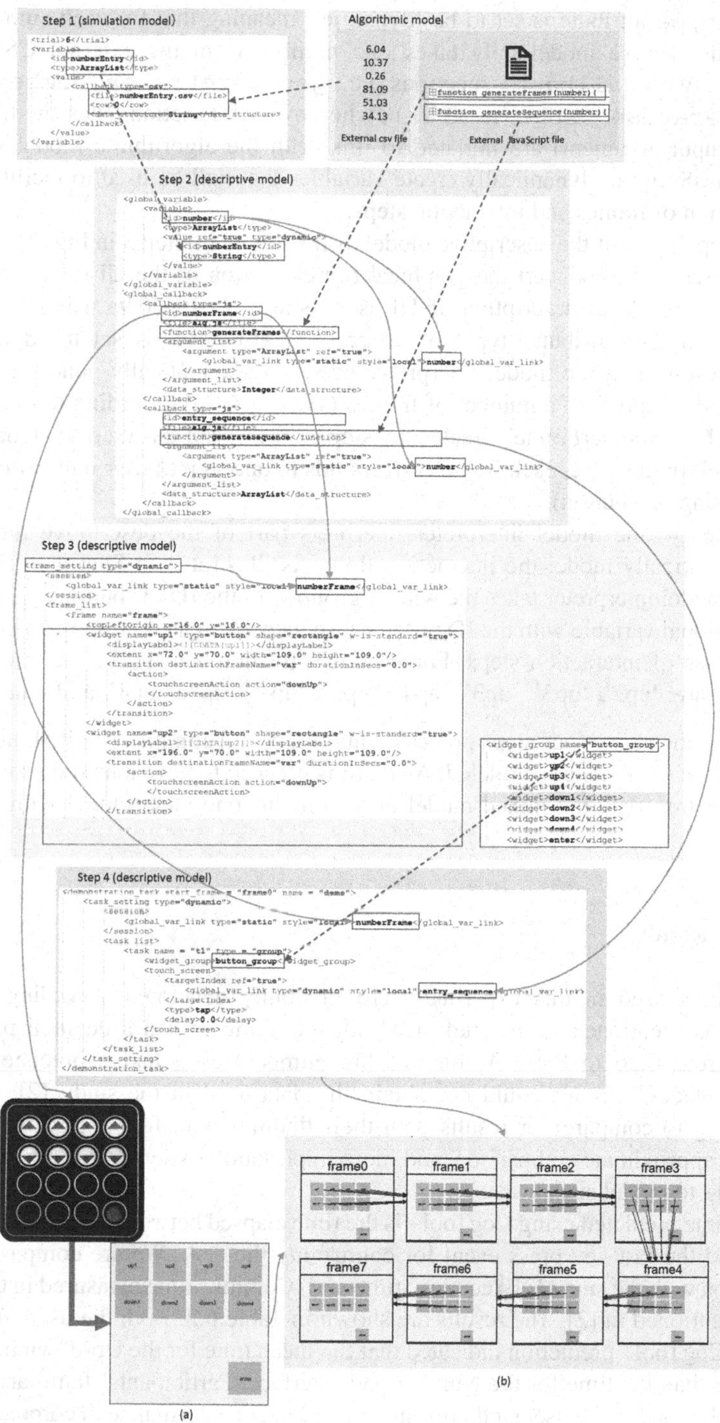

Fig. 6.9 Steps to model the Up-down number entry interface

The `type` attribute is set to be ‘dynamic’, meaning that for each simulation, the descriptive model only takes one number from the external CSV file. Then, two `<callback>` functions (i.e., `generateFrames(number)` and `generateSequence(number)`, whereby each function takes ‘number’ as the input argument) are initiated to link with the algorithmic model written in JavaScript to dynamically create variables that will be used to facilitate the creation of frames and interaction steps.

(3) In step 3, part of the descriptive model as illustrated in Step 3 in Fig. 6.9 is used to describe and convert the graphical representation of the UI (i.e., Fig. 6.8b) to the high-level description of UI as illustrated in Fig. 6.9a using XML. In addition, the attribute ‘type’ of `<frame_setting>` is set to ‘dynamic’, suggesting that the model interpreter needs to automatically generate a low-level description of a number of frames (see Fig. 6.9b) according to the global variable ‘numberFrame’ created in step 2 using the JavaScript algorithmic model. In this case, each frame corresponds to one step of user interaction (i.e., pressing one button).

(4) In step 4, the model interpreter interprets part of the descriptive model to automatically model the interaction flow. As illustrated in Step 4 in Fig. 6.9, the model interpreter takes the widget group with the ID of ‘button_group’ and the global variable with the ID of ‘entry_sequence’ created in step 2 to generate a series of interaction steps. For instance, for number ‘1.25’, the interaction steps are: ‘up2’, ‘up3’, ‘up3’, ‘up4’, ‘up4’, ‘up4’, ‘up4’, ‘up4’, and ‘enter’.

Finally, the above four-steps process is automatically compiled until all numbers stored in the CSV file are modeled. As there is no need to have a mixed probability model for this task, the mixed model only contains one meta model with weight of 1.

6.3.2.2 Result

30 numbers used in this experiment are randomly generated according to the description mentioned in the study [2], “all the numbers had a decimal part and ranged from 0.26 to 83.3. A third of the numbers used had a precision of 2 decimal places.” As we could not obtain the data used in the study [2], we are not aiming to compare our results with their findings with fine alignment, but to make an approximate comparison, and more importantly to demonstrate how to use CogTool+ to model such tasks.

The time predicted using CogTool+ is the time elapsed between the first key press event and the last key press event for confirming the task. We are comparing the prediction with the sum of ‘Execution’ time and ‘Commit’ time measured in the user study mentioned in [2]. The results are shown in Table 6.2. Both the user study [2] and the CogTool+ prediction indicated that the mean time for the Up-down interface is slower than the time for the Number pad interface. Participants’ familiarity with the Number pad in the user study resulted in a greater performance in comparison to

Table 6.2 Mean for the number entry time (milliseconds)

	Number pad	Up-down
User study [2]	2810	5344
CogTool+	2659 (293)	3228 (727)

the other interfaces [2], suggesting that participants could be considered as skilled users. As CogTool+ is used to model skilled users, it is not surprising to find out that the mean time for the Number pad interface is similar between the user study and the CogTool+ simulation. This could also explain the relative large disparity of mean time for the Up-down interface between the user study and the simulation.

6.4 Software Evaluation Discussion

In this chapter, we showed three examples of how to use CogTool+ to model different systems at large scale. We demonstrated that our approach can produce simulated data that are similar to the findings emerged from real human-user studies.

The use of CogTool+ to model these tasks requires less effort compared with conducting real human user studies. Modeling with CogTool+ is less time-consuming and less financially expensive than real human user studies, which often require ethics approval, participants recruitment, experiment design, and data collection. Moreover, the proposed CogTool+ could be considered as a potential contribution to the CogTool research community to provide an alternative way for conducting large-scale modeling tasks. The rest of this section summarizes the advantages of using CogTool+ to model the 6-digit PIN entry task, the Undercover system, and the number-entry task, respectively:

1. Using existing software tools such as CogTool to model 50 6-digit PIN entry tasks involves designing 50 different models manually. By contrast, it only requires a mixed model, a meta model, and a simulation model to model the task using CogTool+.
2. Using existing software tools to model an even more complicated case such as Undercover at the same scale (i.e., 600 models and simulations) requires more work from the user. It is necessary to design 600 scripts to represent 600 models. Each one has to consider the dynamic elements such as pass image selection, challenge screen arrangement, hidden response and public response generation, etc., and the dependent relationship between these elements. Moreover, other factors such as randomness of the UIs, and external data driven process (i.e., visual-search strategy) make the modeling process even more complex. By contrast, it is easier to use CogTool+ to model Undercover at large scale. Each meta model shown in Fig. 6.10 represents one specific model mentioned in Sect. 6.1.1. The algorithmic model and simulation model are shared with all meta models to automatically generate intermediate cognitive models and compile the simulation tasks. Only one mixed model is needed in this case to describe the relationship

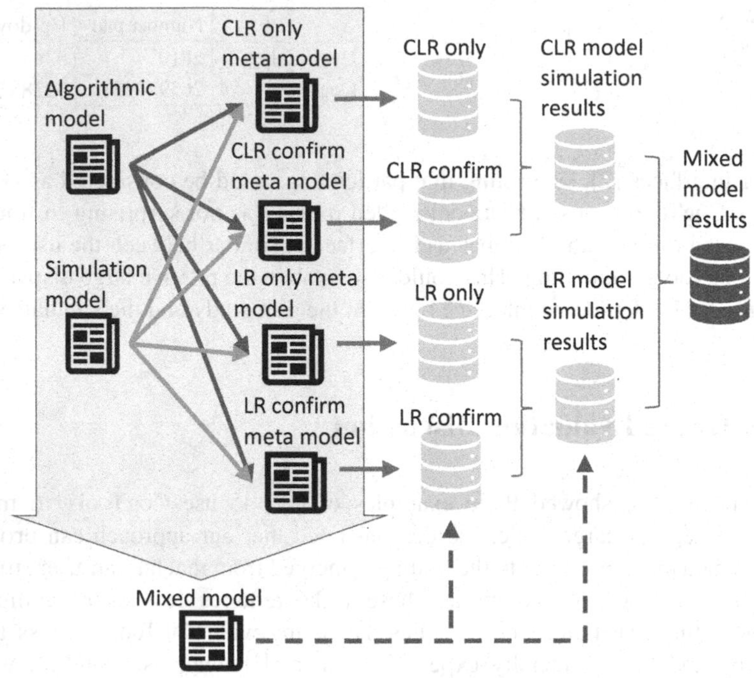

Fig. 6.10 Models designed for the simulation of the Undercover system

between these meta models and assign a weight to each of them. For a user that is familiar with CogTool+, it requires less than 10 min to design all models (including the algorithmic model, the simulation model, all meta models, and a mixed model). CogTool+ can complete the simulation process within a few minutes.

3. Modeling several entry tasks using the Up-down interface manually would entail a heavy workload, as interaction steps are dynamically determined according to the number. With CogTool+, we demonstrated the use of external data in CSV format and an algorithmic model written in JavaScript to achieve the fully automation of cognitive model generation and simulation by means of only one mixed model, one meta model, and one simulation model. Furthermore, this example showcases how to use CSV-based external data and a JavaScript-based algorithmic model together to facilitate the modeling process by means of CogTool+.

References

1. Liu, X., Li, Y., Deng, R.H., Chang, B., Li, S.: When human cognitive modeling meets pins: user-independent inter-keystroke timing attacks. Comput. Secur. **80**, 90–107 (2019). http://www.sciencedirect.com/science/article/pii/S0167404818302736

2. Oladimeji, P., Thimbleby, H.W., Cox, A.L.: A performance review of number entry interfaces. In: INTERACT (2013)
3. Perković, T., Li, S., Mumtaz, A., Khayam, S., Javed, Y., Čagalj, M.: Breaking undercover: exploiting design flaws and nonuniform human behavior. In: Proceedings of the Seventh Symposium on Usable Privacy and Security, pp. 5:1–5:15. SOUPS '11. ACM, New York (2011). https://doi.org/10.1145/2078827.2078834
4. Sasamoto, H., Christin, N., Hayashi, E.: Undercover: authentication usable in front of prying eyes. In: Proceedings of the SIGCHI Conference on Human Factors in Computing Systems, pp. 183–192. CHI '08. ACM, New York (2008). https://doi.org/10.1145/1357054.1357085
5. Woodman, G.F., Chun, M.M.: The role of working memory and long-term memory in visual search. Vis. Cogn. 14(4–8), 808–830 (2006). https://doi.org/10.1080/13506280500197397
6. Woodman, G.F., Luck, S.J.: Visual search is slowed when visuospatial working memory is occupied. Psychon. Bull. Rev. **11**(2), 269–274 (2004). https://doi.org/10.3758/BF03196569
7. Yuan, H., Li, S., Rusconi, P., Aljaffan, N.: When eye-tracking meets cognitive modeling: Applications to cyber security systems. In: Human Aspects of Information Security, Privacy and Trust: 5th International Conference, HAS 2017, Held as Part of HCI International 2017, Vancouver, July 9–14, 2017, Proceedings. Lecture Notes in Computer Science, vol. 10292, pp. 251–264. Springer, Cham (2017)

Chapter 7
Conclusion and Future Work

Abstract This book reviews and explores the applications and implications of cognitive models and related software modeling tools in the HCI field and a particular application area – cyber security. To facilitate the modeling process, the incorporation of human behavioral data (i.e., eye tracking data) is also introduced in this book. In addition, by addressing the issues and challenges of using existing approaches to conduct large-scale cognitive modeling tasks, this book present a conceptual framework CogFrame and a research prototype CogTool+ developed on top of the proposed framework. Further examples of using CogTool+ to model dynamic and complicated UIs are also presented in this book to demonstrate its effectiveness and usefulness.

7.1 Summary of Key Findings

The following points recap this book and present the summary of key insights of each chapter:

- **Chapter 2** presents a brief overview of cognitive architectures including ACT-R, SOAR, EPIC and CLARION, and a brief overview of cognitive models including GOMS, KLM, and CPM-GOMS.
- **Chapter 3** presents a review of three widely used open source cognitive modeling software tools: CogTool, SANLab-CM, and Cogulator. In addition, some examples are given to demonstrate how these tools have been used by researchers and practitioners. This chapters ends with some identified challenges of using existing tools to model human performance. In summary, these challenges include (1) automation of cognitive modeling tasks; (2) flexibility of changing values for some operators; (3) capability of modeling dynamic UIs and user tasks; (4) possibility of interfacing with external data to guide the modeling process.

H. Yuan et al., *Cognitive Modeling for Automated Human Performance Evaluation at Scale*, Human–Computer Interaction Series,
https://doi.org/10.1007/978-3-030-45704-4_7

- **Chapter 4** briefly presents an overview of the integration of human behavioral data (particularly eye tracking data) into the cognitive modeling. Then two user studies are presented to offer insights of utilizing eye tracking data to understand human behavior. The first user study of using eye tracking data reveals that participants have different visual search patterns that can offer insights to help modeling a relatively complex user authentication system 'Undercover'. The second user study investigates the visual search behavior in the context of a simple graphical user authentication task using *emojis, faces, elementary shapes*. The results suggest that participants could complete simple user authentication tasks fastest when the *emojis* were used, and they were slowest when using *faces*.
- **Chapter 5** presents a new conceptual framework for supporting large-scale cognitive modeling. The proposed framework adopts a "plug-and-play" approach that is flexible and re-configurable to interface with existing software tools, cognitive models, and external data to address those issues and challenges identified in Chap. 2. In addition, this chapter also reports our work of developing and implementing CogTool+ – a research prototype by following the proposed framework and extending the cognitive modeling tool 'CogTool'. The design and implementation of CogTool+ can shed light on UI/UX design recommendations/guidelines for developing more advanced software tools to support the proposed framework, such as software tools to support more cognitive architectures and models beyond what are currently supported in CogTool.
- **Chapter 6** presents the evaluation work of using CogTool+ to model three dynamic UI systems at relatively large scale. The results reveal that CogTool+ can generate simulated data that are similar to the findings obtained from real human user studies. In addition, the modeling process of using CogTool+ proved less time-consuming and less financially expensive compared with current practices using CogTool. CogTool+ could be a valuable addition to the HCI community to offer an alternative way to conduct large-scale modeling experiments.

7.2 Future Work

We have demonstrated that CogTool+ (and the general framework CogFrame) is effective and useful to model dynamic UIs at large scale. However, there are some limitations and challenges we would like to call for more research in the future.

- **Making algorithmic models and descriptive models more user friendly**
  As mentioned in Chap. 5, the algorithmic model and descriptive model can be used to facilitate the parameterization and automation of the modeling process. In our current implementation, JavaScript and the use of CSV format are the main ways to work with the algorithmic and descriptive models. It would be less usable for users to design both models from scratch. To release the burden and provide more options, we plan to develop a number of JavaScript reusable utility modules

to assist the users. In addition, some JavaScript based behavioral templates were used in the example presented in Chap. 6 to facilitate the modeling process. We also have plans to build more JavaScript based behavior templates.

- **Full support of CogTool**
  CogTool has full support of the classical windows, icons, menus, pointer (WIMP) user interface. In our current implementation, CogTool+ is prioritized to support basic interaction tasks. There are a number of UI features such as 'context menu', 'web link', and 'pull down list' that CogTool can model, but CogTool+ currently does not support. As our objective is to make CogTool+ fully compatible with CogTool, we will develop more software modules to extend CogTool+'s capabilities to fully support modeling WIMP UI in our future work.
- **CogTool+ GUI**
  We would like to design and develop a comprehensive GUI for CogTool+ in our future work in order to enable researchers and practitioners without any programming skills to use CogTool+.
- **Building an open source community**
  It is our wish to build an open source community co-evolve CogTool+ into a much more comprehensive tool box supporting not just more features of CogTool but also more other cognitive modeling tools, cognitive models and architectures.

Printed in the United States
By Bookmasters